HARMONY OF BABEL

HARMONY OF BABEL

PROFILES OF FAMOUS
POLYGLOTS OF EUROPE

KATÓ LOMB

Translated from the
Hungarian by Ádám Szegi

Edited by Scott Alkire

TESL-EJ Publications
Berkeley, California & Kyoto, Japan

Originally published in Hungary as *Bábeli harmónia (Interjúk Európa híres soknyelvű embereivel)* by Gondolat, Budapest, in 1988. Copyright © 1988 Gondolat.

All footnotes are by the translator and editor except where noted.
The translator and editor thank Dr. Maggie Sokolik and
Dr. Karin Kitzing for their support and contributions.

Copyediting: Hunter Greer and Brian Taylor
Production editing: Mark Handy

Library of Congress Cataloging-in-Publication Data
Lomb, Kató, 1909–2003
Harmony of Babel : profiles of famous polyglots of Europe / Lomb Kató;
translated from the Hungarian by Ádám Szegi

2nd English edition, 2018

English edition copyright © 2013, 2018 Scott Alkire

Library of Congress Control Number: [forthcoming]
ISBN 978-1-5323-6611-6

I. Szegi, Ádám. II. Title.

Cover: *El Jaleo,* John Singer Sargent, 1882

TESL-EJ Publications
Berkeley, California & Kyoto, Japan

10 9 8 7 6 5 4 3 2 1

Contents

≈

Editor's Preface

≈

IN 1957 the linguist, translator, and polyglot Eugene Nida wrote, "Some people do learn a great deal *about* foreign languages in classrooms, but they rarely learn the languages" (p. 43).

The multilingual interpreter Kató Lomb and most of the 21 polyglots[1] she surveyed for *Harmony of Babel: Profiles of Famous Polyglots of Europe* would agree. One of the questions she asked her peers (and herself) was, "What method did you use to learn languages?" Fifteen credited extensive reading, extensive conversation, immersion in the target language community, keeping a language-learning notebook, and dialogues—but not participation in language classes. Otto von Habsburg simply replied, "Not in the classroom." Only five polyglots endorsed language classes, and then only in conjunction with other methods.[2]

Studies of successful learners by Kitzing (1981), Stevick (1989), Krashen and Kiss (1996), Erard (2012), Sykes (2015),

---

1. No fixed definition of polyglot exists, but many researchers agree that a person fluent in three languages (including his or her mother tongue) can be considered a polyglot.
2. The original Hungarian edition of this book does not include answers to this question from two of the polyglots Lomb surveyed.

and Hyltenstam (2016) largely support Lomb's findings; such proficient learners tend to become good at their languages *outside* the classroom. Lomb notes, "Institutions and schools generally cannot provide the concentrated instruction required for the well-paced acquisition of a language." Today the internet, with its many websites, apps, and YouTube channels dedicated to language learning, can give even more of the "concentrated education" that ordinary institutions and schools cannot.

Lomb's query about a language-learning method is but one of nine broad questions she asked her fellow polyglots about language and language learning. In response to her other eight questions, her peers reveal many common language-learning strategies, attitudes, and traits. These qualities appear as well in studies of other multilinguals. It is thus proposed that these commonalities should be allowed to augment, qualify, or challenge current second language acquisition (SLA) attitudes and theories about language learning.

Do "good language learners" exist?

Although it would appear that "good language learners" exist by virtue of the fact that polyglots exist, Naiman, Fröhlich, Stern, and Todesco, in their classic monograph *The Good Language Learner* (1978), write "The study as a whole suggests that *the* successful or good language learner, with predetermined overall characteristics, does not exist" (p. 224). Unfortunately Naiman and his team did not study polyglots. In 1981 Professor Karin Kitzing of Lund University in Sweden, perhaps recognizing this omission, surveyed 76 highly proficient learners from 22 countries and 18 native languages to "confirm or reject some existing hypotheses about language learning." On average the participants were highly advanced in two languages beyond their native languages. Kitzing's highly proficient learners show common characteristics, language-learning strategies, and attitudes, for example:

- The belief in the greater importance of motivation over aptitude and general intelligence in language learning. (In Kitzing's group, 75% considered motivation very important compared to 37% for language aptitude and 15% for general intelligence.)
- The belief in the greater importance of exposure over instruction. (Sixty-five percent of Kitzing's respondents considered exposure to the target language very important in learning the language, but only 37% learned "their best non-native language in a formal setting, at school or university.")
- The ability to monitor performance in the new language
- Field independence: the ability to perceive the structure (pattern) of the new language. (Forty-one percent of Kitzing's subjects said they perceive structure very easily.)
- Extroversion (The majority of Kitzing's subjects considered themselves extroverts.)
- Empathy (Only one person of the 76 surveyed reported having no empathy at all.) [Lomb]
- Self-esteem (None reported having low self-esteem.)
- Tolerance for ambiguity

(pp. 104–6, 108)

Kitzing's study of polyglots was one of the first of its kind. Significantly, many of the beliefs, strategies, and characteristics she identified in her subjects appear in the 22 polyglots Lomb surveyed (including herself) for this volume. These similarities also appear in studies and case histories by Stevick (1989), Chang (1990), Erard (2012), Krashen (2014), Sykes (2015), and Hyltenstam (2016). Does this fact make the term "the good language learner" valid, perhaps even scientifically valid? Krashen (2014) writes, "Case histories can indeed be valid forms of scientific research" (para. 2). Krashen adds that "We [researchers] will ask, in each case, whether the experiences described are consistent with central hypotheses about language acquisition and, most important, whether some hypothesis [sic] are consistent with all cases, while others are consistent with some but not others. Of course, for a hypothesis to be valid, it must be consistent with all cases" (para. 3). Stevick (1989) writes, "[Successful learners'] statements are in fact data...[and] whenever there is an apparent inconsistency between one of these statements and a given [SLA] theory, then the theory must either show that the statement should not be taken seriously, or it must show how the statement is in fact consistent with it after all, or the theory must modify itself accordingly" (pp. xii–xiii).

By these criteria, it appears that "good language learners" do exist, and that polyglots qualify as such.

Challenging SLA theories and attitudes

If we accept that the "good language learner" is scientifically valid, and that polyglots who learn languages (as opposed to acquire them) are highly accomplished learners, we must then ask why polyglots tend to be ignored in SLA research. Could it be because their views in aggregate sometimes challenge SLA theories and attitudes? Although Krashen and Kiss (1996) and Alkire (2005) have shown how Lomb's strategies for language learning largely align with SLA theories, the strategies of polyglots overall often do not. For example, Lomb and Kitzing's polyglots express a surprising indifference to formal language instruction, as do several polyglots studied by Stevick (1989), Chang (1990), Erard (2012), Krashen (2014), Sykes (2015), and Hyltenstam (2016). Lomb's polyglots also express views that challenge current attitudes in SLA concerning the value of good pronunciation and multilingualism.

Regarding pronunciation, Lomb asked her interviewees, "Which is the most important language skill: grammar, vocabulary, or good pronunciation?" The inclusion of "pronunciation" in a question about language skill is rather bold; pronunciation has been neglected as a language skill in SLA studies since at least the 1960s.[3] (Perhaps not coincidentally, it is generally considered impolitic in most discourse communities to draw attention to a learner's non-standard pronunciation, not to mention a peer's or a superior's.)

Though round-table participants Felix and Toulouze allow that serviceable pronunciation will suffice in most real-life situations, Lomb, Taneda, and Naumenko point out that being able to pronounce a language properly has undeniable advantages. Lomb writes, "In language, experience has shown that pronunciation contributes to *appearance* and *appeal*. Pronunciation is decisive in the first moments of a conversation; it is on pronunciation that you base your judgment of your partner's language skills." Taneda reports that "I perhaps react the most intensely to pronunciation mistakes. A foreign-sounding accent hurts my ears like a song hummed out of tune." Naumenko reminds us that "A native will not understand you, even with the right choice of words and exact grammar, if your pronunciation is distorted. The goal, criterion, and cornerstone of language skills is the ability to communicate."

---

3. See *Pronunciation in the Classroom: The Overlooked Essential.* Ed. by Tamara Jones. Annapolis Junction, MD: TESOL Press, 2016.

Naumenko's comment may be more relevant today than it has ever been. With more people worldwide speaking English as a second language than as a first language, and with globalization increasing, the ability to converse in *standard* English will allow speakers of non-English first languages to communicate more effectively. The stakes can be high. For example, universities in the U.K. and U.S. now have many professors who speak English as a second language teaching students who speak English as a second or even third language.

Lomb also asked her group, "What is multilingualism good for?" As with pronunciation, this question is seldom asked in academia. (If it is, it is not taken seriously or is answered with the usual bromides.) The answers Lomb received vary considerably. Otto Back reports, "My job—directing the administration of the Interpreting School in Vienna—requires me to deal with multiple languages. I consider multilingualism counterproductive from the point of view of quality. To use a primitive metaphor: If a cat chases 10 mice at once, it will catch fewer than by chasing only one." Géza Képes offers, "A great advantage of polyglottism is that you can access many pieces of literature first-hand."[4] For his part, Gedeon Dienes says, "In my opinion, it is not worth knowing more than two languages 'actively.'" András Sugár states, "In my profession, language skills are worth gold. I have done reporting in 80 countries, and I do interviews in 10 languages...I know of only one pleasure greater than the command of languages: learning them." But this pleasure is not universal. Possemiers flatly asserts, "If you are an interpreter, [multilingalism] is good for nothing. You have to deal with your selected main language so much

---

4. It is estimated that only 5% of the non-English books currently published worldwide are translated and published in English.

that you have no time to use other languages. And even then you cannot keep up with the constant increase of vocabulary in your main language!...In our profession, it actually breeds mistrust when someone speaks too many languages." In essence Lomb's polyglots tell us that the greatest value of being multilingual, aside from personal satisfaction, is the degree to which it enriches and expands one's work, reading, and personal life. Otherwise the return is minimal for the time invested, or even, as Possemiers claims, a negative, at least professionally.

Other reasons why polyglots are ignored

As noted earlier, polyglots have been generally neglected in SLA studies. One reason may be because their views of language and language learning sometimes challenge SLA theories and attitudes. Other reasons exist as well. McLaughlin (1987) believes that "Recourse to conscious or unconscious experience is notoriously unreliable and hence cannot be a source of testable hypotheses about the learning process" (p. 152). Aurélien Thomas (2015), in reference to Krashen's seminal text *Principles and Practice of Second Language Acquisition* (1982, 2007), notes that what is obvious to "bilingual/polyglot people" regarding language learning is "ignored by traditional teachers and formal educational systems" (para. 2). Van Doren (1991) recalls a blithe dismissal issued by an academic toward bilingual people: "Being bilingual doesn't mean you know anything about language" (p. 185). However, Scovel (2001) sees the value of both experimental and experiential data for understanding successful language learning: "The evidence [of successful language learning] can be either experimental or experiential. Given the complexity of SLA, I think we need a lot of both" (p. 10).

Some linguists acknowledge polyglots but propose only general, unsupported approaches to them. Chomsky advocates this strategy: "The only way to deal with the complexities of the real world [i.e., multilinguals] is by studying pure cases [monolinguals] and trying to determine from them the principles that interact in the complex cases" (in Grosjean, 2013, para. 9). However, linguists such as Erard, Hyltenstam, Kitzing, Krashen, Sorenson, Stevick, Sykes, and Wilton have taken a different tack. They have studied and compared the "principles" (to use Chomsky's word) of *polyglots* (not monolinguals) to see what they reveal about successful language learning. Wilton (2015) writes, "Applied Linguistics should...continue and enforce the investigation of multilingual biographies and multilingualism" (p. 70). *Harmony of Babel* is such an investigation.

Summary

Although polyglots by definition are highly successful language learners, SLA researchers have seldom studied them. It is proposed that polyglots' views regarding language and language learning should be considered in order to augment, qualify, or challenge current SLA attitudes and theories. As we have seen, surveys of polyglots by Lomb and Kitzing reveal that these master learners express indifference toward formal learning, believe in the importance of standard pronunciation, and are divided on the value of multilingualism. Lomb's polyglots also augment, qualify, and challenge dominant SLA views on

- When we can say we know a language
- Why we fail at learning a language
- The influence of age on language learning

- The value of knowing Latin and Esperanto
- The relative "values" of languages
- Sorting multiple languages in our minds

In addition to its round table of polyglots, *Harmony of Babel* presents capsule biographies of historical polyglots, a short essay on what characterizes the good language learner, and a view of why language instruction (circa 1988) was failing in Hungary. Finally, this second edition includes an interview Dr. Lomb gave to Hungarian TV in 1974, newly transcribed and translated by Ádám Szegi.

Scott Alkire
The California State University
July 2018

References

Alkire, S. (2005, Fall). Kató Lomb's strategies for language learning and SLA theory. *The International Journal of Foreign Language Teaching.*

Chang, C. (1990). *How I learned English.* Taipei: Bookman Books Ltd.

Erard, M. (2012). *Babel no more: The search for the world's most extraordinary language learners.* New York, NY: Free Press.

Grosjean, F. (2013, May). Noam Chomsky on bilingualism. *Psychology Today.* Retrieved from https://www.psychologytoday.com/blog/life-bilingual/201305/noam-chomsky-bilingualism

Hyltenstam, K. (Ed.). (2016). *Advanced proficiency and exceptional ability in second languages.* Boston/Berlin: De Gruyter Mouton.

Kitzing, K. (1981). The good language learner. *Lingua, 3,* 104–108.

Krashen, S. D. (1982, 2007). *Principles and practice in second language acquisition.* Hemel Hempstead, U.K.: Prentice Hall International.

Krashen, S. D. & Kiss, N. (1996). Notes on a polyglot: Kató Lomb. *System, 24*(2), 207–210.

Krashen, S. D. (1997). *Foreign language education the easy way.* Culver City, CA: Language Education Associates.

Krashen, S. D. (2014, June). Case histories and the comprehension hypothesis. *TESOL Journal.* Retrieved from http://www.sdkrashen.com/content/articles/skrashen_case_histories.pdf

Lomb, K. (2008, 2011). *Polyglot: How I learn languages.* Trans. K. DeKorne & Á. Szegi. Berkeley, CA: TESL-EJ Publications.

Lomb, K. (2016). *With languages in mind: Musings of a polyglot.* Trans. Á. Szegi. Berkeley, CA: TESL-EJ Publications.

McLaughlin, B. (1987). *Theories of second-language teaching*. New York: Edward Arnold.

Naiman, N., Fröhlich, M., Stern, H. H., & Todesco, A. (1978). *The good language learner*. Clevedon: Multilingual Matters Ltd.

Nida, E. A. (1957). *Learning a foreign language: A handbook prepared especially for missionaries* (rev. ed.). New York, NY: Friendship Press.

Scovel, T. (2001). *Learning new languages*. Boston: Heinle & Heinle.

Sorenson, A. (1967). Multilingualism in the northwest Amazon. *American Anthropologist, 69*(6), 670–684.

Stevick, E. W. (1989). *Success with foreign languages*. New York, NY: Prentice Hall.

Sykes, A. H. (2015). The good language learner revisited: A case study. *Journal of Language Teaching and Research, 6*(4), 713–720.

Thomas, A. (2015). [Review of the book *Principles and practice in second language acquisition*]. *Language Tuition*. Retrieved from https://mrthomaslanguagetuition.wordpress.com.

Van Doren, C. (1991). *A history of knowledge*. New York, NY: Ballantine.

Vitray, T. (1974). Interview with Dr. Kató Lomb. *Ötszemközt* [Between Five Eyes]. (Between you, me, and the camera). Budapest.

Wilton, A. (2015). Multilingualism and foreign language learning. In *Handbook of foreign language communication and learning*. Ed. by Knapp, K., Seidlhofer, B., & Widdowson, H. Boston/Berlin: De Gruyter Mouton.

Introduction: The Sun Is Shining

≈

IT IS NOON; the fog has lifted. The blue tapestry of the sky gleams above us cloudless, and we state with a smile: The NAP[5] is shining.

The same fiery star illuminates the land of the Botocudos in South America, but it is only about to rise there. The descendants of the German settlers who migrated there still call it the SONNE.

Dusk is approaching in Odessa. The hot rays of the COHLIE[6] are reflected on slowly thickening mist drops.

In Mexico City, it is five in the morning. As indicated by the pale radiation, the SOL will soon be rising above the horizon.

The neon signs of geisha houses have just lit up in Tokyo. Their lights obscure the sun's descent behind the viaduct of Ginza. The sun here is named TAIYŌ.

In New Zealand, the SUN has long sunk below the waves of the ocean. The clock atop the Wellington Town Hall shows 11 PM.

The five billion inhabitants of our planet Earth have called

---

5. Sun (Hungarian).
6. Sun (Ukrainian); pronounced "sontse."

19

this glowing celestial body several thousand different names. A multilingual is a person who has managed to fight his way through this confusion of Babel. They are the ones this little book is about.

Of course, many worthy citizens live in the Land of Polyglottia. I have chosen 21 clever multilinguals. I tried to choose colleagues I could interview in person, but I didn't want to restrict my choices to those living in nearby countries.

I was driven by two criteria during the selection: those who had acquired *active* speaking skills in at least eight languages and those who had acquired this knowledge by *study*. This is why several excellent compatriots of mine are not included in this volume. I also excluded people who only translate or revise texts, and those who owe their multilingualism to circumstances of their birth or to coincidences in their lives. Allow me to explain.

There are not only multilingual people but multilingual nations. The nations usually became multilingual as a result of their geographic location or historical development; their inhabitants did not study, so to speak, the languages they acquired. These polyglots were not of interest to me.

Similarly, there are quite a few people who became multilingual by unavoidable personal reasons. An old hand and star in my profession, simultaneous interpreting, is Denis Deschamps, age 85. He was born in Germany to a French father and a Russian mother. His fate carried him to Greece, where he attended English-language schools. No wonder he speaks five languages better than many natives. I envied him, I wondered about him, but I didn't ask him my questions concerning my obsession—language-learning efficiency. I knew that he couldn't provide any experience or guidance. He did not methodically "obtain" his languages; he "picked them up."

Language pedagogy in English differentiates between conscious *language learning* and instinctive *language acquisition.* Deschamps, with all the vicissitudes of his life, picked up almost all his languages the same way a child learns his or her native tongue. His knowledge was a result of the environment in which he lived. All he needed to do was drift along in the various linguistic streams.

His fate is an extreme case, but our century, rife with storms, has made many people at least bilingual. It is enough to think of the millions living near former borders or transferred to other countries as children. A language acquired under such circumstances is sometimes called a "second native language" in the technical literature. People do not learn it out of interest, but out of self-preservation. For them, to learn a second language is a necessity. To my subjects, learning languages is a luxury, as they put it.

We would, of course, make a mistake if we were to draw a sharp line between artificial and natural ways of language acquisition, calling "natural" whatever was picked up from one's surroundings, and "artificial" whatever one obtained through study. The two ways cannot be strictly separated from each other.

Most of my interviewees professed that they grew up in a completely monolingual environment. However, all of them spent some prolonged time in foreign countries later on. Though some of my subjects did pick up foreign languages as youths, they polished their knowledge through conscious study.

The fact that someone or something can be named in several different ways is discovered by most children in kindergarten. They discover that they are not only Punkin or Lil Bro, but David Jones or Sarah Richardson. At the same time the mother tongue also changes and develops. Many expressions fall out of young people's vocabulary naturally, even those still in use by older generations. I admit that in lectures I sometimes hesitate to use old terms, such as "prima donna." I don't know if teenagers have ever learned them.

I interviewed my subjects for almost a year, orally and in writing, to find out if they have a "trick" that enables their achievements in language learning.

Among my original candidates, schedule conflicts made some unavailable for interviews. With others, I simply didn't succeed. A famous polyglot asked me not to visit him at his home in Paris because he is always so busy there! Instead, he wanted me to meet him in Helsinki on October 15. He was going to give a lecture there, and "Helsinki is just a stone's throw away from Budapest, anyway." An F grade in geography, Professor!

There were people who shirked the term "polyglot" because of excessive modesty, and they didn't help me get closer to my goal, which was to discover the traits that characterize the Good Language Learner.

Polyglots: Old and New

≈

ACCORDING TO THE BIBLE, it was in the land of Shinar where Babel's curse struck humanity. Ever since then, there have been people who haven't resigned themselves to their linguistic isolation and have kept trying to open the locks of foreign languages. In the mist of the past, reality and likelihood are distorted by myths. It can be assumed that the heroes of myths and legends owe their polyglottism mostly to their high positions, rather than to their skills.

Instead of newspapers, television, and radio, in heroic times there were bards and minstrels spreading the news of the world. They were the ones who satisfied the masses' thirst for information. Travelers from far away were free to talk big. It is no wonder that these bygone reporters endowed the heroes of their songs with amazing physical and spiritual capacities. The heroes' wisdom and bravery that conquered lands was often supplemented by a miraculous mastery of languages.

Common people's imaginations have always been captured by the lives of great achievers. Our age is no exception. We are eager to glance behind the painted or printed scenes to learn about a person who stands in the glare of a million eyes.

Although minstrels used to exalt the strength, intellect, and character of their heroes, the well-informed in our jaded age strive to deglorify our achievers. "Have you heard that the actor XY was arrested for driving under the influence? That NN didn't write his bestseller himself but found it among the papers of a fellow writer? That the pop singer PQ will get divorced again even though two women are already suing him for child support?"

It is sweet to hear and even sweeter to forward this news; these stories are almost as unverifiable as oral traditions in mythic times.

The credibility of religious founders and prophets was greatly enhanced if they were portrayed as able to preach and decline the Word in countless languages.

In the Old Testament, Rabbi Eliezer credits Mordecai with having the command of 70 languages. Although the Buddha's language is not known, it's likely that he taught in a variety of Middle Indo-Aryan dialects. Mohammed is praised by some sources (Prideaux, Russell) for knowing multiple languages.

On the other hand, the Ancient Greek era wasn't favorable to polyglottism. Plato was enthusiastic about Eastern philosophers, but he was not willing to learn their languages. He considered the knowledge of languages slave wisdom. Similarly, Themistocles didn't learn Persian until his exile, and out of boredom. Contempt for the languages of the defeated was part of the arsenal of all conquerors. The Normans despised the English language, and later the English despised the Celtic languages.

However, this linguistic illiteracy apparently didn't apply to kings and emperors. Mithridates was said to speak 25 languages, according to Aulus Gellius. Plutarch [in *Plutarch's Lives*] extols Cleopatra's knowledge: "She spoke most languages, and there were but few of the foreign ambassadors whom she answered through an interpreter." In his *Natural History*, Pliny documents the intellectual excellence of Cleopatra's old admirer, Julius Caesar, as follows: "We find it stated that he was able to write or read and, at the same time, to dictate and listen. He could dictate to his secretaries four letters at once and on the most important business; indeed, if he were busy with nothing else, he could dictate as many as seven."[7]

Rome's masters pounced on Greek language and culture with the greed of the nouveau riche. It was a matter of prestige to speak Greek, just as knowledge of Latin conveyed status in the early 20th century. Roman senators had the right to speak Greek even in the Senate. The Greek language survived the fall of Hellas: The first inscriptions on Christian catacombs were in Greek.

I think it was the aversion of Hellas's inhabitants toward foreign languages that gave rise to the profession of interpreting. Herodotus reports that the Greek ports swarmed with traders from Asia Minor, Babylon, Scythia, Arabia, and Libya. Each had to have his own Greek-speaking dragoman [interpreter]. Greeks were not willing to learn the language of even their most important customer, Egypt.

The interpreting profession flourished in Roman times as well. Pliny the Elder notes that merchants in Dioscurias, Colchis [today Sukhumi, Georgia] represented 300 different tribes, and the Romans employed 130 interpreters for business transactions.

When the Roman Empire dissolved, relations between East and West declined.

Attila the Hun (406–453) is said to have dictated a law pro-

---

7. Caesar spoke Classical and Vulgar Latin and possibly Greek.

hibiting the use of Latin in the regions he conquered in Italy. He imported slave teachers who further weakened the defeated enemy by spreading the language of the Goths.

During the Middle Ages and the Renaissance, our polyglot ancestors thrived in two areas: religious debates and trade. In the first, clergymen with conflicting views on issues strove to convince each other. Some clergy spoke in Greek, some in Latin, and others in Hebrew. Paul the Apostle encouraged our interpreting profession. In his first epistle to the Corinthians (14:27) he recommends, "If anyone speaks in a tongue, let there be only two or at most three, and each in turn; *let one interpret.*"

The greatest linguaphile[8] of the Renaissance age, Pico della Mirandola, learned French, Hebrew, Latin, Greek, and Chaldean (in addition to his native Italian) in order to spread his belief that Christian mysticism was rooted in the Kabbalah. At the age of 18, he allegedly gave lectures on church law in 22 languages. He made so many enemies that 10 years later he resigned his rank of count, and he decided that he would wander the world as a barefoot preacher. However, he died of fever at the age of 31 in Florence.

The Scotsman James Crichton, known as Admiral Crichton, lived one century later. Not only could he claim the knowledge of 12 languages, but he also played several instruments well and won competitions in fencing, long jumping, and riding. In addition, he was well-versed in theology. He advocated for his tenets at the universities of Paris and Padua and stated that he was ready to challenge anyone not sharing his views in Syriac, Hebrew, Arabic, Greek, Latin, Spanish, Italian, English, German, Flemish, and

---

8. Instead of the term *linguist*, Lomb uses *linguaphile* for those who learn languages as a vocation or hobby, acquire languages with the goal of actually using them, love them, learn them easily, and speak them well.

Slavonian.[9] His life was short; he was killed at the age of 22 in a street brawl.

The other reason for the boom in interest in foreign languages was the increased speed of ships and the acceleration in the exchange of goods. Foreign-trade clerks and executives who, apart from Venetian, spoke Neapolitan and Palermitan (for example) became in demand. However, political tyranny and religious intolerance also contributed to the spread of languages. Greeks expelled by Muslims from Constantinople, and Moors and Jews made homeless by the Spanish Ferdinand and Isabella, took the tongue of the old homeland with them (and handed it down to their children and grandchildren).

Felix of Ragusa was not an outcast: King Matthias of Hungary, who reigned from 1458–1490, lured him to his castle in Buda[10] so that Felix could help enrich the treasures of the king's library with his knowledge of Italian, Greek, Latin, Chaldean, Arabic, and Syriac. I am proud of a contemporary of his, the musician H. K. Freher, who spoke 36 languages and all his life claimed to be Hungarian. He was said to sing French romances, Maltese serenades, Eastern Orthodox hymns, Spanish madrigals, German *Lieder*, Hebrew psalms, and Styrian folk songs with equal perfection. His vocal range was also uncommon: It extended from basso profundo to falsetto.

Jan Amos Komenský (1592–1670) was the last bishop of the Unity of the Brethren in Bohemia and the first apostle of modern language education. Whether he actually translated his own books—written under the name Comenius—into Arabic, Per-

---

9.   Slavonian is probably Croatian.
10. Before their unification as Budapest, Buda and Pest were independent cities on opposite sides of the Danube River.

sian, and Greek (as well as another 12 European languages) is difficult to ascertain today, but it is a fact that he was the first to protest against the then-dominant pedantic way of language teaching. He demanded that practical sentences be included in course books and that texts intended for reading be supplemented with illustrations. Our children today, who turn the pages of their picture books and tear them apart when bored, do not know that they owe thanks for this delight to the brave innovation of a pious priest, born almost four centuries ago.

Beginning in ancient times, and for two millennia, it was the rank of a king, a prophetic calling, or the zeal of missionaries that impelled people to formally learn foreign languages. A new era was heralded when academic interest took over the role of motivation. Heroes of this age are entitled to have a place in the Pantheon of Polyglot Polymaths. These days only encyclopedias preserve encyclopedic knowledge. Two or three centuries ago it was possible for Leibniz to be a poet, linguist, lawyer, and mathematician, for Alexander von Humboldt to be philosopher, botanist, theologian, and explorer, and for Alexander's brother Wilhelm von Humboldt to be a literary critic, diplomat, and philologist.

I thought of them with envy the other day when I asked an eminent computer scientist how to translate a technical term from his field.

"How should I know?" He shrugged. "You see, I work in software, not hardware."

I could also quote the physiologist, an associate professor at a research institute, whom I tried to question about what we know about the cerebral localization of various mental activities (such as memorizing foreign words).

"Oh, don't ask me about that," he replied. "Such things are to be found in the cortex. My area is not that but the mesencephalon (midbrain)!"

Gottfried Wilhelm Leibniz (1646–1716) was orphaned at the age of six, and from that time on he trained himself in languages. He started to learn Latin from a work by Livy. At 12, he wrote poems in this language and took up Greek. He was admitted to the faculty of law at the University of Leipzig at the age of 15. In 1666, the degree of doctor was conferred on him—albeit through connections, due to his young age—and he was even offered a chair at the University of Altdorf. However, he was more attracted to philosophy, politics, physics, mathematics, and theology. He wrote his doctoral dissertation in Latin, his historical treatises in English, and his books on theology in French. He agitated in German for rapprochement toward France.

Alexander von Humboldt (1769–1859) was a polymath as well. He described the flora of the mines of Freiberg in Latin, presented Galvani's muscle experiments in German, and made geographical and meteorological observations on the Orinoco and Amazon rivers with a French scientist, Aimé Bonpland. Later he lived at the court of Frederick William III in Potsdam and, with the Russian government and the Duke of Sussex, then president of the Royal Society, he succeeded in setting up magnetic and meteorological stations in Russia and England. He initiated organizing the "scientific conspiracy" of nations, which A. M. Clerke called one of the noblest fruits of modern civilization.

Karl Wilhelm von Humboldt (1767–1835) was a Prussian Minister of Education, a minister (envoy) at Rome, and a distinguished scholar. He translated a tragedy by Aeschylus into German and was the first to describe the Basque language. He discovered the ancient Kawi language of Java and, according to many, was the founder of the philosophy of speech as a discipline.

However, the most outstanding linguistic figure of the 18th century was Mikhail Lomonosov (1711–1765), the first professor of chemistry in Russia and a historian, philosopher, poet, and natural scientist. He lectured on physics in Russian yet could articulate in Latin the principle of conservation of matter to no less a scientist than Leonhard Euler.

Yet he did not have a high opinion of Latin. He was proud that his native tongue had not derived from Latin but—as he believed—from Greek. There was also some religious intolerance lying behind the linguistic zeal of this Eastern Orthodox scientist. "The Poles converted to Catholicism long ago and celebrate mass in the vulgar Latin of the Dark Ages and from generally bad authors. We (Russians) got better religious writing through Greek.

"In Slavic languages, we can see the splendor of Greek, from which we can improve upon the richness of Russian, which is already marvelous. Therefore Russian is capable of accepting the beauty of Greek through the agency of Slavic languages." (Misley & Gazda, 1982, p. 280).

Of course, what he meant here by Slavic languages is the Old Slavonic text of Church books. However, as a poet and a stylist he believed that Russian should only keep the Old Slavonic terms that are understandable and currently in use (based on Misley & Gazda, 1982, pp. 282–3). It was due to Lomonosov that the Russian literary language was born. Belinsky called him the Peter the Great of the Russian language.

According to records available at the Academy of Sciences in Saint Petersburg, Lomonosov knew 27 languages. Beyond the better-known ones, he knew Latvian, Estonian, Ancient Greek, Turkish, Tatar, Serbian, and even Hungarian.

It was after the death of Lomonosov that Giuseppe Mezzo-fanti, the shining star of polyglottism, appeared.

Cardinal Giuseppe Mezzofanti (1774–1849)

"Infinite is the trouble and small the profit of studying a language in such a manner that the reasoning faculties remain idle, and the memory is merely loaded with strange words and their combinations. The study becomes less wearisome, and more useful and dignified, when the teacher judiciously calls attention to the structure of the idiom, pointing out the principles that regulate its innumerable variations, but especially dwelling on that which governs them in the largest point of view, and may be said to bear the rule in the language and constitute its leading property..."

(Watts, 1859, pp. 247–8)

Ferenc Pulszky (1814–1897) was a young aristocrat who traveled all over Italy in his youth. In his travel journals he vividly described his visit to Rome. He was lured to the Eternal City by the desire to find in the Vatican the copy of the Golden Bull, issued by King Andrew II,[11] which was sent to the Pope. Alas, the precious document had vanished when Pope Urban V temporarily moved from Avignon back to Rome in 1367.

The young aristocrat found solace in the artistic treasures of the city. The pomp of the Church rituals absolutely dazzled him. Pulzsky (1880–2) wrote, "Among the lines of soldiers, the silver-covered papal dragoons sped along, and then came the violet-covered bishops, archbishops, and cardinals, each followed by his own caudatarius bearing the train of the purple robe. Twelve scarlet-clad servants carried the golden throne, on which the Pope sat

---

11. Issued in 1222 in Hungary, often compared to the Magna Carta in the history of England.

dressed in white, pleated wool, with a wide red velvet collar and a golden tiara on his head. He was accompanied by a servant on either side with a large white peacock-feather fan, and then came the Swiss Guards with halberds and in red and yellow medieval garments" (1958, p. 86).

Mezzofanti, whose fame had reached even distant Hungary, is nowhere to be seen in this luxuriance of colors and lights. Pulszky (1880–2) went to the Vatican library searching for the cardinal and was received by a short, thin priest stooping over old manuscripts. When the priest learned that his visitor was Hungarian, his eyes lit up behind his spectacles. "He addressed me in Hungarian, moreover with a thick Debrecen accent that he had learned from a Hungarian hussar.... He greatly encouraged me to dedicate myself to linguistics, for only the first 20 or 24 languages involve some difficulty—that was his comment—and the rest are then very easy" (1958, p. 87).

Mezzofanti, beaming with educational optimism, was at the time of Pulszky's visit already the pride of the Vatican. His significance was not due to the high rank he had achieved in the Church hierarchy; rather, it was his talents which enhanced the splendor of his rank.

Yet, it is not possible to imagine this scholar outside the framework of the Church. In this age, one of the major sponsors of cultural research was the papacy.

The haughty patricians' wealth was increased by the yields of cornfields, the cargoes of seafaring galleys, and the tax pennies of citizens, but these riches began to disperse as power was passed from one generation to the next. Those belonging to the Church remained together and kept growing. The heads of Roman, Venetian, and Florentine distinguished families were compelled to think in terms of a single generation; in the hourglass of the Church, eternity itself was running. *Patiens quia aeternus* [Patient because eternal], Augustine said when asked why God tolerates the sins of humans.

The old age of consuls and governors is marred by their successors' power-hungry impatience; the respect for a priest only increases with the passage of time. Pius IX was celebrated as a "young pope": He was 54 at the time of his election. He headed the Roman Catholic Church for more than 30 years.

The Greek word *katholikos* means universal or comprehensive. A prerequisite of universality in religion is that the teachings of the faith reach as many people as possible. The knowledge of foreign languages, which facilitates the spreading of the faith, ranked high among the values embraced by the Church. For example, it was recorded about Pope Pius XII that he kept a diary in secret code and in various languages as secretary of state of the Vatican, and then as pope, for 40 years. After his death, the precious document disappeared from Castel Gandolfo, the summer residence of popes.

I cherish a nice personal memory about the effectiveness with which the Church teaches foreign languages.

One of the Vatican staircases is guarded by young attendants in picturesque apparel. Their uniforms have been unaltered for centuries: a wide black beret, a striped jacket with loose-fitting sleeves, and a ruffled, white collar. They stand still and unshaken in front of the chattering crowd snapping their cameras.

However, if someone should venture beyond the permitted line, one of these statue-like guards comes to life at once and politely advises the uninformed tourist to leave. This happened to a young Japanese man who had gleaned from a guidebook that various publications are sold at the *libreria*. Thinking that *libreria* [bookshop] was the same thing as *biblioteca* [library], he eagerly tried to enter the Biblioteca Vaticana to buy postcards to send to Tokyo.

One of the young guards explained in very good Japanese the difference between the words *libreria* and *biblioteca*, and then he froze again.

Edited by the *Tipografia Poliglotta Vaticana*—i.e., the Vatican Polyglot Press[12]—some apostolic briefs are published in 45 languages.

The ability to adapt to different times is part of the success of spreading the faith. There are surprisingly modern paintings exhibited in the Vatican Museum, such as works by Oskar Kokoschka and Salvador Dalí. Even the science of telecommunications has its own patron saint. Archangel Gabriel became its heavenly representative, as he was the one who transmitted the Annunciation.

Mezzofanti, the little boy with special gifts, was taken under the wing of the Church, which fostered intellectual values. The Church was where the greatest polyglot of all times grew world-famous. He was called a living Pentecost even during his life.

We, his successors, are of course interested in the way he acquired his mastery of languages, which remains unsurpassed. Unfortunately, he had little to say to those who questioned him about it. His biographer C. W. Russell[13] (1858) notes that he considered his talent a gift from God, who gave him "an excellent memory...an incredible flexibility of the organs of speech" as well

---

12. Renamed the *Tipografia Vaticana,* or Vatican Press, in 1998.
13. All references to Mezzofanti are from Russell (1858) unless noted or qualified otherwise.

as "a quick ear." He was also known for the "almost instinctive facility with which, by a single effort, he grasped all of the principal peculiarities of the structure of each new language."

His pious answer is well suited to a priest, but it cannot be used as a methodological guide. At most his answer defines the four faculties that are still thought of as the fundamental pillars of successful language learning.

I did not find a note referring to musical interest on his part, but Russell mentions the *sensitivity of his ears* often: He was able to perceive and reproduce sounds and stresses in their most delicate shades. His ability to imitate rivaled that of the best actors. When he was in high spirits, he could speak Latin, his professional native tongue, for hours in a "German" or "Russian" accent.

His visual memory was as good as his auditory prowess. The Bolognese priest and naturalist Ranzani noted that on one occasion he wanted to quote from a book that was hidden in a dark corner of the library. He was still trying to light a candle when his fellow priest appeared with the desired folio. Mezzofanti had fished it from the depths of the library in a minute.

It would be easy to sigh and say, "Of course, he just has a knack for languages." But it is proven by statements by and about Mezzofanti that, apart from his special gift, he *studied* indefatigably as well. In fact, he studied to the point of drudgery and plodding, as reported by his biographer. True enough, with his eminent analytic faculties he was quick to recognize the rules that build sounds and letters into words, and words into sentences. But even as a cardinal, he was not reluctant to visit his pupils every day, from whose lips he hoped to acquire living and reliable knowledge.

The German theology professor Friedrich August Tholuck

asked him in 1829 how he started learning a language. Russell writes, "His own way of learning new languages was no other than that of our schoolboys, by writing out paradigms and words, and committing them to memory." And: "He was able to concentrate all his faculties upon any language that he desired to pursue, to the exclusion of all the others that he knew." Gogol, who spent 12 years in Rome, met him several times. Gogol described Mezzofanti's method as follows: "He selected a sentence, reflected upon it for a long time, and turned it over in all directions. He did not proceed to the next one until he gleaned from it all that he wanted to know" (Annenkov 1960, p. 101). Russell reports that "With such diligence, usually 14 days were sufficient for him to learn how to understand and speak a language."

Russell notes that there was a pile of dictionaries, catechisms, books, and "vocabularies" on his desk.[14] When he went to confess or visited his relatives, he murmured and translated poems on the way. "I use every minute for studying," he said with gentle self-mocking irony, "just like a musician who composes even during walking, except my fingers are not moving."[15] The famous jurist d'Aguesseau was once asked when he had written one of his most valuable works. D'Aguesseau replied, "During those hours when my wife was late serving dinner."[16]

What we know for certain is that Mezzofanti never acquired his knowledge on location. He never crossed the border of Italy. Of the Italian cities, he knew only Bologna, where he was born, and Rome, where he lived for 40 years until his death. On only

---

14. "Vocabularies" probably means "glossary."
15. Probably based on Russell, pp. 476–8, although not attributed there to Mezzofanti himself.
16. Probably based on Russell, p. 476.

one occasion was he compelled to travel in a thirst for knowledge, and that was to Naples. At that time the only Chinese missionary in Italy lived there. The 57-year-old Mezzofanti paid him a visit and became his student. He revealed to his fellow priests that he struggled more with Chinese than with any other language. Whoever studies a language that uses characters instead of letters will have to learn that these languages consist of a distinct "eye-language" and "ear-language."

Mezzofanti developed the basics he had learned from the Chinese missionary to such perfection at home that he was later able to deliver sermons in the missionary's Cantonese dialect.

We are not Mezzofantis, but I would like my language-learning friends to ponder his example for a while. Too many like to think that a foreign language can be truly learned only abroad.

It is for their benefit that I recall the case of a representative of a completely different academic field. Jean Baptiste d'Anville, the famous French geographer, discovered that maps created prior to the mid-18th century were often the figments of imagination and were swarming with errors. He corrected wrong data on 211 drawings and in 78 academic articles, and he was the first to draw an authentic map of Europe after the fall of the Roman Empire. He accomplished it all by sitting in his study, and without ever crossing the border of Paris.

What Mezzofanti expressed about his own language-learning method shows genuine modesty—that of a well-balanced person who pursues his chosen discipline with pleasure. Mezzofanti was recorded to have prolonged conversations with himself in the absence of a partner. "The faculties of the mind chiefly employed in acquiring language [are] perception, analysis, judgment, and memory." "When one has learned 10 or a dozen languages essentially different from one another, one may, with a little study and attention, learn any number of them."

Mezzofanti studied the structure of languages, but in terms of their character and rhythm, he preferred to rely on his ear. "I learned Flemish from a native of Brabant, and this is the way I pronounce the word; but you, from Flanders, pronounce it thus."

The story of his life reveals more about his methods of studying than his succinct remarks. Unfortunately, the data are sometimes uncertain and occasionally conflicting.

The lack of data did not bother some publishers in 19th-century Europe. Russell notes that the French publisher Le Bel once commissioned one of its authors to write a book about the life of the English poet Robert Southey (1774–1843). The person in charge objected, having hardly any data available about the life of the poet. "It doesn't matter," Le Bel answered. "Write it anyway, embroider it! Make it all the more colorful. What matters is the *embroidery*, not whether it is true or not."

I will not comply with this guidance. I will stick to the truth that I managed to cull from various records.

Giuseppe Mezzofanti was born in 1774 in Bologna, at 1988 Via dei Malcontenti, the child of a poor carpenter. Out of six sons and seven daughters, it was only he and his sister Teresa, 10 years his senior, who survived. His father wanted him to be a tradesman and intended to leave his humble workshop to him, so that he could later support his mother and his sister. At six, Giuseppe was already sitting at the bench, though his job was only to collect the scattered shavings.

In 1780 a hot summer arrived in Bologna. The heat of the workshop became intolerable; they dragged the bench out to the street. The little boy became aware of the Latin and Greek words coming from the windows of the nearby school. Teachers were trying to make the poor pupils of the inner city repeat the classical texts. They did not seem to succeed very well. The six-year-old carpenter's apprentice, who didn't even know the alphabet of his own language, became so irritated by the ignorance of the students that he shouted up the correct form after each mistaken word.[17]

The old priest who taught the class hurried down to the street to chase away the troublemaker. When he caught sight of the scrawny little boy, short even for his age, he is said to have carried the "prompter" up the stairs, much to the amazement of teachers and students.

Filippo Cicotti, the head of the school, was astounded at the talent of the child and immediately found his father. However, Cicotti failed in persuading the old carpenter that the gifted boy had to be put through school; the father, who was tired of work, insisted on keeping the child by the workbench. Not until the Scuole Pie, the board of the Piarists, offered a free education did the carpenter acquiesce in Giuseppe's acquiring "grammar, geography, writing, arithmetic, algebra, and the elements of Latin" as a resident student.

Among the teachers of the Scuole Pie at Bologna were many Jesuit priests who had been expelled from Spanish territory. Apart from the classical languages, the young student acquired two versions of Spanish: Mexican and South American. He had an instructor of German as well, Father Thiulen, a Swedish Jesuit also forced to emigrate to Italy.

---

17.   Probably based on Russell, p. 129, which states that "young Mezzofanti... caught up every Greek and Latin word that was explained in the several classes."

At the age of 17[18] he was admitted to the Archiepiscopal Seminary of Bologna, but his sickly and meager build compelled him to three years' rest. When he regained his strength, he became familiar with the "Jewish grammar" and then the Coptic, Arabic, Syriac, and Syrian Chaldean languages, in addition to mastering his regular school subjects.

The American writer J. T. Headley recorded a touching story about Mezzofanti as a novice priest in the north of Italy. Mezzofanti was called to a jail at the outskirts of Bologna, where two sailors found guilty of piracy were waiting to be executed the next day. Mezzofanti tried to make himself understood, but to no avail. He was overwhelmed with grief that these men should leave for the other world without the benefit of confession and absolution. It was then that he founded the method that would govern his later language learning.[19]

He had the prisoners recite the Ten Commandments, the Lord's Prayer, and the Apostles' Creed.[20] Based on the known texts, he probably found not much difficulty in recognizing the most important words he needed for a confession—such as heaven, God, temptation, resurrection, hell, sin, virtue, forgiveness, and judgment. His sensitive ears identified from the context even the rules that linked the words into sentences.

If the events of the late 18th century hadn't interfered, his life

---

18.   According to Russell, p. 137, it is more likely to have happened as early as 1786, at age 12.

19.   According to Russell, pp. 129–30, "He returned to his room and resolved to acquire the language before morning. He accomplished his task, and the next day rendered their confessions in their own tongue!" (This anecdote suggests that Mezzofanti had developed his famous method earlier.)

20.   Lomb mentions Hail Mary as well, but Russell adds: "or any one of those familiar prayers which are the common property of all Christian countries."

would have taken the same course as those of his predecessors who had inhabited the monasteries. However, the serene tranquility of those "cognizant of the infinity of the Almighty above the finiteness of life"[21] would hardly have urged him to copy sacred texts and paint the initial letters of the pages. As it happened, this Bolognese priest devoted his life to collecting linguistic knowledge and comforting the dying.

The bloody turn of the century plunged him into the thick of life. Napoleon's army clashed with Austrian troops in the territory of Italy. The war raged in front of the walls of Bologna. Grenades exploded on the stones of the streets, and houses burned in jets of flames. Life came to a halt in the besieged city.

The fortunes of war sometimes favored one party, sometimes the other. Bologna was filled with wounded Austrian, German, French, Czech, Polish, Croatian, Hungarian, Ruthenian, Slovenian, and Romanian soldiers. Mezzofanti tirelessly visited the hospitals and first-aid stations. He confessed, absolved, and gave communion.

One cannot help but be moved by the thought of the young and fragile priest wandering the ripped-up streets and ministering to the wounded out of devotion to his discipline. After becoming familiar with their languages, he would console the soldiers with the power of their mother tongue.

Modern psychoanalysis searches mysteries of the soul. It tries to recognize and heal the problem with a prolonged and complicated investigation. The consolation provided by the Church is simple and unambiguous. *Ego te absolvo*—I absolve you. The poor country lads that Mezzofanti met, driven to foreign lands

---

21. Author's note: Quote from Attila Vári.

and tormented by the fear of death, must have found it a relief that they could give their confessions in their native tongues and understand the consolations of a priest.

Mezzofanti's biographers record that there was a Roma person among the wounded soldiers. Mezzofanti's command of languages was then supplemented with another, Zingaro.[22]

In 1797, Napoleon proclaimed the Cisalpine Republic in Bologna. The meek young priest refused to take the oath of allegiance.

In 1806, Napoleon shuttered the library where Mezzofanti had been cataloging Arabic manuscripts. From the silent world of folios, he found himself out on the street for good, but not on the barricades. Apart from his vocation as a priest, his poor health disqualified him for military resistance. But with gentle resolve he rejected the repeated invitations of the victorious general to leave war-devastated Bologna, move to Paris, and put his skills to the service of France.

Napoleon liked to see himself as a patron of the arts and sciences. He approached three major figures of Italian intellectual life: Volta, Galvani, and Mezzofanti. He called on the physicist Volta at his laboratory in Pavia, witnessed his experiments, and tried to lure him to Paris with the promise of money, rank, and title. Napoleon also made Luigi Galvani, the physician, physicist, and philosopher, a similar offer. Galvani stayed in Italy and died of starvation during the siege.

Napoleon tried to win Mezzofanti over through intermediaries. However, Mezzofanti declined the persuasion with diplomatic modesty: "I feel that the shade suits me best. Were I to go to Paris,

---

22. Russell refers to this incident on pages 154, 239, 244, 248, and 345 and uses the word Gipsy; Zingaro is simply its Italian equivalent.

I should be obliged to set myself up upon some candlestick, where I should give out only a faint and flickering gleam, which would soon die utterly away."

He remained in Italy and supported his sister and her children by giving lessons. He was attached to them with the bonds of the traditional Italian family. He taught modern and classical languages to the scions of the Pallavicini, Ercolani, and Marescalchi families. At the same time, he carried on with his own studies; he practiced the languages he knew and set about learning Sanskrit.

In 1815 the Napoleonic wars ended, and Pius VII returned to Rome. Mezzofanti was given a chair again: He taught Oriental languages and Greek. His fame attracted more and more admirers to Bologna.

At this time Italy was becoming again a center of intellectual life in Europe. To stabilize their thrones, crowned heads hurried there to create ties with each other and the papacy. The relieved aristocracy drew inspiration for beautifying their palaces with the arts of past ages. The most renowned writers and artists convened as well in this citadel of classical culture.

Monarchs, nobles, and princes of poetry did not fail to pay their respects to the world-famous linguist in the Eternal City.

Where popes Pius VII and Leo XII failed, Pius VIII succeeded; Pius VIII managed to lure Mezzofanti to Rome in 1831. There he worked first as a canon of Santa Maria Maggiore. In the Maronite convent he perfected his knowledge of ancient and modern Syriac, Armenian, Turkish, and Persian. Then he received a select assignment: teaching future missionaries at the *Congregatio de Propaganda Fide,* or Congregation for the Propagation of the Faith.[23]

The Congregation, housed in a magnificent building located on the way to the Janiculum,[24] was founded by Pope Gregory XV in 1622. This was the residence for missionaries in training. The resurgence of missionary work was made especially timely by two circumstances. On the one hand, it was the way for the papacy to counter the spreading of the Reformation; on the other hand, the dynamism of European colonization had exposed new territories ripe for the promotion of religion. Rivalry between the individual orders—Dominicans, Augustinians, and Franciscans—also played a role in raising the standard of evangelism. Each of them strove to mobilize the most talented "cadres" as possible for the spread of their respective orders.

Students for the Congregation were recruited from promising youths from India, Oceania, and North Africa. The first prefect was Gregory XV himself. Since its inception in 1622, 18,000 missionaries have been trained there, including 6,000 from overseas. Mezzofanti managed 114 students from 41 countries. He learned from them and taught them.

He focused his attention on languages that he hadn't encountered before. The first was Hindustani. He was also interested in the differences among the dialects of the indigenous people of North America. In his notes he describes the exotic lessons he garnered. For example, he writes that the sound "b" was entirely missing from the dialect of a particular student from Africa. As he was searching for the reason, it turned out that members of that African tribe wear a heavy pendant in their lips; therefore they cannot pronounce labials.

---

23.   Called Congregation for the Evangelization of Peoples since 1982.
24.   A hill in western Rome.

It must have been this period of his life when the never-ending master and never-ending pupil were the happiest. With smiling modesty he received the gratitude of his students and of the nobles who arrived in Rome. Some visitors' notes are worth citing. They say more than any official biographical data about this man who was superhuman in knowledge, but quite human and even childlike in behavior. Independent of the chronological order and the rank of those who met him, I have selected some reports that reveal his learning methods and the level of his knowledge of languages.

The Emperor Francis I visited him in 1819, in Bologna. The Austrian monarch seems to have doubted Mezzofanti's skills. Francis's entourage included German, Hungarian, Czech, Romanian, Croatian, and Polish courtiers. When the courtiers in turn addressed the host in their native tongues, and Mezzofanti replied in the same language to each with "perfect fluency and correctness," Mezzofanti achieved "not merely approval but admiration and applause" from the Emperor.[25]

A Hungarian, Baron Zach, had the opportunity to meet Mezzofanti in 1820, accompanied by the Russian prince Volkonski. The two aristocrats, both amateur astronomers, were attracted to Bologna by the solar eclipse, due on September 20. Mezzofanti addressed Zach first in Hungarian, then in German (namely the "Saxon, Austrian, and Swabian dialects"). The Hungarian changed the conversation in jest to Romanian. Mezzofanti continued in the same language and, in fact, with such pace that his partner implored: "Gently, gently, Mr. Abbe; I really can't follow you; I am at

---

25. Russell, on p. 231, refers to the people as "German, Magyar, Bohemian, Wallachian, Illyrian, and Pole." "Illyrian" may refer to a Croatian today.

the end of my Latin-Wallachian."[26] Of course, Mezzofanti spoke Russian with Volkonski, at such a level that the prince admitted, "He should be very glad if his own son spoke it as well."

"The annular eclipse of the sun," Zach wrote, "was one curiosity for us, and Signor Mezzofanti was another."

The German scholar Guido Görres joined the company of Mezzofanti's adherents in Bologna. Görres was an accomplished linguist himself; he learned Persian to translate an 11th century national epic by Abu'l-Qāsim Ferdowsī. He depicts Mezzofanti as a man of astounding knowledge, and at the same time "good-natured, conscientious, indefatigable." He had "a childlike simplicity and innocence" and was ready to show his skills anywhere to anyone. He was happy to improvise pious verses in the "assigned" language upon request, without preparation. Mezzofanti was not proud of his rank: "It is not as a cardinal that I go there [to the House of Catechumens[27]]; it is as a student—as a youth."

He always spoke unpretentiously about his multilingualism. One of his visitors quoted Charles V as saying, "As many languages as a man knows, so many times he is a man." Mezzofanti replied, "Well, that ought rather to humble us; for it is essential to man to err, and therefore, such a man is the more liable to error."

One his most illustrious guests was Nicholas I, "the Sovereign of all the Russias," who came to Rome in 1845 to visit Pope Gregory XVI. It was commonly said at the time that the interpreter between the two potentates was Mezzofanti. Extemporizing distiches [couplets] would not have sufficed there. The pontiff reproached the Tsar for the treatment of Catholics in Russia.

---

26. Wallachian is a dialect in southern Romania.
27. Youngster or convert waiting baptism/confirmation.

Mezzofanti had to employ all his diplomatic aptitude so that this member of the Holy Alliance could leave Rome contentedly.[28]

The cardinal, so lenient and benevolent with everyone, was recorded to have made one critical remark. The Tsar changed the language to Polish—maybe to reduce the tension or to flaunt his skills. Mezzofanti was said "to have taken some exceptions to the purity, or at least the elegance, of the Emperor's Polish conversational style."

An anecdote that quite illuminates Mezzofanti's method of learning was recorded on the occasion of King Oscar of Sweden's visit to Italy. The ruler, then Crown Prince, addressed Mezzofanti in Swedish, and Mezzofanti replied in the same language "quite perfectly." The prince then suddenly changed the conversation into a dialect unique to one of the provinces of Sweden. Mezzofanti was obliged to confess his inability to understand him. However, in a subsequent interview, the priest began speaking in this very dialect! "From whom have you learned it?" exclaimed the prince. "From your Royal Highness," replied Mezzofanti. "Your conversation yesterday supplied me with a key to all that is peculiar in its forms, and I am merely translating the common words into this form."

Another nice story is associated with Lady Blessington. This lady, surprisingly adventurous compared to other women in those times, visited quite a few countries in Europe, including Italy. However, somehow she lost her way in the Vatican and was desperate to find someone to ask for directions. She became aware of a conversation in English. She turned to the speakers, relieved. "You can't imagine what a delight it is to come across a country-

28. Probably based on Russell, p. 443.

man," she said to Mezzofanti. He saluted her graciously and said that, though not a countryman, he would gladly help her rejoin her party. "You speak English perfectly yet are not an Englishman!" The Lady was astonished. "Then you can be no other than professor Mezzofanti?"

The cardinal won over Lord Byron, too: as a scholar, a sage, and a human being.

"I don't remember a man amongst them [the literary men] whom I ever wished to see twice," wrote the poet, famous for his cynicism, "except perhaps Mezzofanti." "I tried him in all the tongues in which I knew a single oath or adjuration to the gods, against post-boys, savages, Tartars, boatmen, sailors, pilots, gondoliers, muleteers, camel-drivers, vetturini, post-masters, posthouses, post, everything. And egad! He astounded me—even in my English."

"I can go no further," admitted the noble poet. "Pardon me, my Lord," rejoined Mezzofanti, and he proceeded to repeat a variety of London slang, up to then unknown to Byron. The Abbé Gaume recalls the story in his book *Les Trois Rome.*

Byron not only presented the priest with a copy of his famous *Childe Harold's Pilgrimage,* but also improvised a poem in his honor, based on a satire by Donne:

> "You prove yourself so able,
> Pity you was not druggerman [dragoman] at Babel!
> For had they found a linguist half so good,
> I make no question but the Tower had stood."

Let me retell the meetings of two Hungarian noblemen with the cardinal.

Baron Glucky de Stenitzer—who, in Ferenc Pulszky's opinion, only usurped his title—visited Rome in 1845. Mezzofanti not only addressed him in impeccable Hungarian, but also used four dialects of the guest's language: "the pure Magyar of Debreczeny, that of the environs of Eperies, that of Pesth, and that of Transylvania!"[29]

In 1817, the cardinal met the most notable visitors from Hungary. The palatine Archduke Joseph called upon him in the Magliavecchia library in Bologna, along with the chamberlain, Fidél Pálffy, and the seneschal, Count Becker. Mezzofanti saluted them in eloquent Hungarian. Shame of shames: Neither the palatine, nor the two aristocrats, spoke Hungarian. Pálffy tried to ease the awkward situation by answering in a medley of Czech and Polish, as he had picked up a bit of Slavic languages from his serfs on his estate in Eastern Hungary.

On the other hand, Mezzofanti had more luck with Gábor Fejérváry, Ferenc Pulszky's uncle, the famed archaeologist and art collector, with whom he had several long conversations in Hungarian.

Let me interrupt the course of the narration for a moment to insert a sigh that I often hear from my acquaintances of retirement age. "You mean I should deal with foreign languages? But even my neighbor's name or my family doctor's name often escape my memory!" To prove that a diminished *memory of names* does not imply the general decline of mental capacities, I will include here an episode from the second meeting of the cardinal and Fejérváry.

Watts (1859) writes that Mezzofanti welcomed his guest with

---

29. The places in today's spelling are Debrecen (Eastern Hungary); Eperjes (today Prešov in Eastern Slovakia); Pest, the eastern part of today's Budapest, but then a separate city; and Transylvania (today in Romania).

open arms and remembered exactly where and in what circumstances they had met, but he, the greatest polyglot of all time, added, "Sir...you must excuse me for having forgotten your name."

The mechanical memory of names weakened even in Mezzofanti's case, but his language skills that required logical thinking remained until the end of his life. The Cardinal Altieri met the scholar, 73 at that time, in 1847, and he exclaimed in raptures at the end of their conversation: "But you are a living dictionary of all languages!" The cardinal, who was in poor health, replied with melancholy, "What am I but an ill-bound dictionary!"[30]

A gentle and pious man, Mezzofanti died in the same calmness on March 15, 1849, at the age of 74. *Andiamo, andiamo, presto in Paradiso* (Let's go, let's go quickly to heaven) were his last words.

On the wall of the house at 1988 Via dei Malcontenti, a plaque preserves his memory. Its inscription is a Latin distich: *Heic Mezzofantus natus, notissimus Orbi, / Unus qui linguas calluit omnigenas.* (Here was born Mezzofanti, widely known around the world, the one who spoke all the languages.)[31]

Whoever excels will always attract people who envy or criticize them. The only objection such people could make against the amiable Mezzofanti was that he did not create anything lasting in academia. Baron Bunsen, the Minister Resident of Prussia, the head of the Archaeological Institute in Rome, said about him: "Mezzofanti has the keys to all human knowledge, but he makes no use of them" (Watts).

---

30. Perhaps based on Russell, p. 395.
31. The first line of the epitaph exists in several versions: *Heic ortus Mezzofantus, notissimus orbi; Heic Mezzofantus patrite stupor ortus et orbi;* and *Hic est ille vir, hic toto memorabilis orbe.*

His lack of interest toward theoretical philology generated critical comments even from his admirers. "A giant as a linguist, Mezzofanti certainly was a child as a philologer," Russell writes. Russell met the cardinal in 1843, when Mezzofanti was 68.

It is a fact that Mezzofanti wrote only one book: his funeral speech at the burial of his early instructor, Emanuel Aponte. Biographers mention that he spent much time on Mayan or Aztec manuscripts and made remarkable statements about their hieroglyphics, about which little was known at the time.

Posterity also knows about a Mezzofanti lecture at the Academy of Bologna in 1816. It dealt with the language in seven municipalities near Vicenza, Italy. The inhabitants of this region were descendants of the Cimbri and the Teutones who had crossed the Alps and settled near Vicenza in the 2nd century BC.[32] The closed community had preserved its original tongue with such miraculous fidelity that when Frederick IV of Denmark visited them in the early 18th century, he was allegedly able to converse with them.

Unfortunately, Mezzofanti's extensive correspondence with the great people of his age doesn't reflect his intellectual brightness. His stilted style, laden with embellishments, was a mixture of the predilection of his age for ceremony and the pomposity of literary language. On the other hand, he was fond of improvising high-sounding, shapely little poems at anyone's request in a matter of minutes, always with some pious content.

Although even his fans were obliged to admit that he did not leave anything lasting to posterity, nobody questioned his linguistic skills. Except for one—a woman.

---

32. Russell, p. 217, mentions "in the year of Rome 640," which, added to 753 BC, gives 113 BC, rather than the 6th century BC that Lomb mentioned.

"He rather studies the words than the subject of what he reads." "The empty, unreflecting word-knowledge and innocently exhibited small vanity with which he was filled reminded me of a monkey or a parrot, a talking machine, or a sort of organ wound up for the performance of certain tunes, rather than of a man endowed with reason."

Needless to say, this person was a Hungarian. What's more, she was an elegant aristocrat, a Mrs. Paget (née Polyxena Wesselényi). Her education seems to have been obscured by Hungarians' tendency to sneer, apparently independent of era.

Madame Paget met Mezzofanti in 1842. In her book *Journey in Italy and Switzerland,* she admits that the cardinal "spoke it [Hungarian] well enough" and that "his pronunciation was not bad." She noted that he read the works of Kisfaludy[33] and Csokonai[34] as well as Pethe's *Natural History.*[35] Maybe it was only her wounded vanity from the following incident that produced her critical words: She had a copy of the Hungarian statesman Miklós Wesselényi's book *On Prejudices*[36] sent to the binder to be handsomely bound in white leather as a present for Mezzofanti. However, when she presented the volume to him, all he said was: "Ah! Very fine, very finely bound. Gilded, beautiful, very fine, thank you very much," and put it away in a bookcase.

Yet, the cardinal's affection toward the Hungarian language and literature was mentioned by every one of his biographers. He reportedly once said to Fedele Mayer,[37] a professor of Hungar-

---

33. This might refer to either of two Hungarian brothers: Sándor Kisfaludy (1772–1844), a poet, and Károly Kisfaludy (1788–1830), a writer and painter.
34. Mihály Csokonai Vitéz (1773–1805), Hungarian poet.
35. Ferenc Pethe (1762–1832), Hungarian journalist and writer on agriculture.
36. A book published in 1833 and banned by the Habsburg government.
37. Fidél Mayer or Majer (c. 1793–1863), parish priest.

ian descent at Modena, that he had always liked the Hungarian language, but since knowing him, he had taken it into his heart even more.

Zachariáš Frankl, the Czech-born poet, paid his respects to Mezzofanti in 1823. The cardinal first addressed him in German. Then, on receiving the guest's introductory letter in Hebrew by Signor Luzatto, the rabbi of Padua, Mezzofanti continued in that tongue. At the end of the visit, Frankl presented him with a copy of his volume of poems, writing the inscription in German: "To Mezzofanti, the Chameleon of Language." "Ha," Mezzofanti said with a smile, "I have had countless compliments paid me, but this is a shiny new one." Then he asked, "Do you know what language I place before all others, next to Greek and Italian, for constructive capability and rhythmical harmoniousness? Hungarian. I know some pieces of the later poets of Hungary, the melody of which took me completely by surprise. Mark its future history, and you will see in it a sudden outburst of poetic genius, which will fully confirm my prediction."

In the same year, on the Hungarian Plain, our great poet Sándor Petőfi was born.

Mezzofanti's contemporaries and successors were keenly intrigued about how many languages Mezzofanti actually "knew."

The quotation marks on *knew* are necessary because—as we will learn from interviewing today's polyglots—the concept of "knowledge" is difficult to define. It is still not easy to draw a line between language and dialect. Drawing a line must have been especially challenging 150 years ago. The underdevelopment of transportation and the lack of mass communication devices must have isolated local dialects from each other to the point of incomprehensibility.

I will quote some of his statements and a few notes of his contemporaries in connection with this matter:

In 1805, at the age of 31, he was "master of more than 24 languages," according to Father Caronni.

In 1817, he "read 20 languages and conversed in 18," according to Stewart Rose.

In 1836, he mentioned 45 languages.

When he was appointed a cardinal in 1838, pupils of the Propaganda Fide[38] greeted him with poems in 53 languages. He answered each of them in the language of the poem, among them Arabic, Ethiopian, and Basque. The chronicles do not mention *which* Basque language. Mezzofanti spoke three of its dialects: the Lapurdian, the Souletin, and the Gipuzkoan.

Before 1839, he used to say that he knew "50 and Bolognese."

In 1842, answering Mrs. Paget's question, he said "I speak only 40 or 50."

In 1846: "Seventy-eight languages and dialects."

It is documented that in 1843, for the festival of Epiphany, he wrote metric odes in 42 languages. The languages included Albanian, Bulgarian, ancient and modern Armenian, Coptic, and classical and modern Chinese.

His nephew, Gaetano Minarelli, may have had a relative's bias when he claimed that Mezzofanti knew 114 languages—though not at the same level of competency. The first category, which Mezzofanti knew *perfettamente* (perfectly), comprises Spanish, French, Portuguese, German, Swedish, Danish, Dutch-Flemish ("Flamingo"), English, Russian, Polish, Czech, Hungarian, Mal-

---

38. Missionary arm of the Catholic Church.

tese, Latin, Greek, Hebrew, Chaldean, Arabic, Coptic, Armenian, Persian, Turkish, Chinese, Syriac, Ethiopic, Amharic, Hindustani, Romanian, and Basque.

Minarelli includes here six dialects of the Italian language: Sicilian, Sardinian, Neapolitan, Lombard, Friulian—and of course Mezzofanti's native Bolognese, which this immensely benevolent priest declared "the ugliest of all the dialects of the peninsula."[39]

(I would read this list of Italian dialects shaking my head if a recent experience of mine didn't testify that they indeed have to be learned one by one. In the early spring of 1986, I was at Pontebba, Italy. Having taken delight in Károly Markó's[40] lifelike paintings—mountain streams plunging down from sky-high cliffs—I resolved to continue my journey by taking the evening express train. All I had to do was find out the departure time and the opportunities to change trains. Unfortunately, the owner of the sole boardinghouse that stayed open heroically during the pre-season could speak only Friulian. I did not understand a word. I couldn't help but spend the night there and proceed toward Tarvisio in the morning.)

It is not a coincidence that the subdivision of a national language into local vernaculars is most conspicuous (and the most frightful for interpreters) in those two countries that were unified late: Italy and Germany. The subject of our admiration, Mezzofanti, records that when he was preparing to confess a seriously ill

---

39. The criteria are: "frequently tested and spoken with rare excellence." The others are Albanian and Serbo-Croatian ("Illyrian"). The last six (Syriac, Ethiopian/Ge'ez, Amharic, Hindustani, Romanian, and Basque) belong to the second group, "stated to have been spoken fluently, but hardly sufficiently tested." The remaining languages are Gujarati, Algonquin, and Californian.

40. Károly Markó Sr. (1793–1860) and Károly Markó Jr. (1822–1891), both notable painters.

Sardinian country girl, he had to spend two entire weeks acquiring her language—a blend of Latin, Italian, and Spanish—as if it were some exotic language.

It goes without saying that the precise number of languages and the level of his knowledge produced the most heated debates among the cardinal's biographers.

Apparently, even cardinals are not prophets in their own countries. Of the four major works that deal with Mezzofanti's life, only one—mentioned above, written by his nephew—came from an Italian's hand. The other three originate from a Frenchman (M. Manavit), an Irishman (C. W. Russell), and an Englishman (T. Watts). The common trait of the four authors is that all of them question the reliability of the others' data.

Russell, in *The Life of Cardinal Mezzofanti* (1858), condemns the "facts" in a lecture given by Watts at the Philological Society in Great Britain, and he denounces Minarelli for including in his list of Mezzofanti's languages such "mystical" tongues, never heard of by anyone, as Braubica, Cahnapana, Emabellada, and Rocorana. In turn, Watts objects that Russell counts the "Debreczeny, Eperies, Pesth, and Transylvanian" dialects separately from Hungarian.[41] (Watts refers to the name of the first city as Debreczin, "which by some oversight is called Debreczeny.") Among other things, he questions that the cardinal spoke Japanese. He writes, "No statement of the kind can stand in stronger need of proof than that the cardinal, who was generally accustomed to study a language from the lips of a native, should be acquainted with Japanese, which probably at the time of his death was not known to three persons in Europe, while in the course of the cardinal's

---

41.   It was actually named Debreczen at that time (today: Debrecen).

whole life and for more than a century before [then], a native of the country had not been seen in Italy" (Watts).

I would like to add one more argument of theirs to these ravings, which are not far in their refreshing malice from the disputes of writers in today's weekly journals. Russell adds Cornish as one of Mezzofanti's languages "studied from books, but not known to have been spoken." As Watts puts it, "Indeed it is hard to imagine to whom the cardinal could have spoken it. According to popular belief, the last person who had a colloquial knowledge of the language was Dolly Pentraeth, who died…in 1778, four years after Mezzofanti was born at Bologna. A monument is now about to be erected in the churchyard of her parish by Prince Louis Lucian Bonaparte, to commemorate at once the death of Dorothy Pentraeth and the death of the Cornish language." (Watts).

At the same time, Mezzofanti's contemporaries ladled out compliments. Watts notes that the Pope called him "a living Pentecost," Meluzzi "a hero of legends," Augustin Theiner "the master of all masters," and Watts "an intellectual prodigy."

I cannot help it: None of the enthusiastic compliments made me understand Mezzofanti's greatness as much as the title he awarded himself when the Imperial Academy of Russia elected him as an honorary member in 1839. The cardinal thanked the Academy for the distinction via a letter in Latin. Only the signature was in Italian:

> "Giuseppe Mezzofanti,
> Cittadino dell' Universale Repubblica delle Lettere"
>
> (A Citizen of the Universal Republic of Literates)

Sándor Kőrösi Csoma (1784–1842)

He was born at the base of Kőröscserje mountain[42] and interred at the foot of the Himalayas. He devoted his life to one belief, which in the light of science proved to be a misbelief. He wanted to claim the conqueror Attila, the Scourge of God, for the Hungarian nation, but Csoma's legacy turned out to be a Tibetan dictionary and grammar, which was the best of its time ("No one managed to create anything more or better"—Giuseppe Tucci[43]).

Before Csoma's recent biographies (by György Kara, Ferenc Szilágyi), his life story was written by Dr. Tivadar Duka, a retired surgeon major of the British Royal Bengal Army. "The power of acquiring languages was the extraordinary talent of Csoma. He had studied the following ancient and modern tongues, and he was proficient in many of them: Hebrew, Arabic, Sanskrit, Pashto, Greek, Latin, Slavonic, German, English, Turkish, Persian, French, Russian, Tibetan, with the addition of Hindustani, Mahratta, and Bengali. His library at his death had a dictionary of each of the languages he was acquainted with, and on all were his manuscript annotations."[44]

Little is known about the order and manner he acquired these languages, and some of the data is contradictory. A relative of his, József Kőrösi Csoma, a Protestant pastor in Monó, recorded that he did not like German, although he had imbibed it with his mother's milk. Despite this dislike, German remained in his extraordinary memory to such an extent that at the University of

---

42. Today in Romania. His village of birth is usually given as Kőrös, renamed later in his honor as Csomakőrös, or Chiuruș in Romanian.
43. Probably from Giuseppe Tucci, *Alessandro Csoma de Kőrös*, 1942.
44. Duka, p. 155. The quotation is from Dr. Archibald Campbell, *Asiatic Society of Bengal*, vol. XIV, p. 823.

Göttingen he spoke the language fluently.

He practiced French conversation in the same city "with a very old lady from Paris," but he used for Italian the method that he would often apply later on: studying literary works. He had good masters: Dante, Tasso, and Boccaccio.

He studied Arabic and Turkish at Göttingen. When he had made "nice progress in Greek literature," he set out to learn English. One of his fellow students recorded in 1818, "I handed my English grammar over to Kőrösi—and my hat, too, as his was rather threadbare." In the cold winter of the next year, Csoma walked to Timişoara and Zagreb "to become familiar with Croatian and other dialects."

He learned Persian at the age of 36. According to his above-cited relative, he learned it perfectly. However, all he noted about his competency was that "I got acquainted with the grammatical elements of the Persian language."

In 1819, he could call 13 living and dead languages his own. Equipped with these, as well as an oilcloth haversack and a stick, he set off for his long journey through the Principality of Wallachia (now southern Romania). During his wanderings, he had to cope with hardships that only one who firmly trusts his strength can endure. However, confidence was coupled in his case with infinite modesty. In Sabathu, India, he had to ask the commander of the border post, Captain Kennedy, for permission to continue his journey. Instead of permitting him to go, the newly appointed Kennedy arrested the "suspicious stranger." Csoma strove to deflect the accusation of espionage by providing a detailed autobiography, and he apologized for his "unrefined style." In a letter to his college, he emphasized only that, "The knowledge of foreign languages has always been a favorite pastime of mine."[45]

Apart from a dazzling memory, his knowledge must have been facilitated by an excellent ear and the ability to imitate. He covered the distance from Aleppo to Bukhara [now in Uzbekistan] sometimes in the robe of an Asian dervish, sometimes in Armenian garb, sometimes in the company of pilgrims or traders. Today native speakers in these parts may smile tolerantly at mispronunciations by infidels, but had Csoma been exposed as one, it would have cost him his life.

It was almost a coincidence that Csoma chanced upon the first Tibetan book, the *Alphabetum Tibetanum.* The structure of this curious language aroused his interest so much that he improved his knowledge with a Persian-speaking Tibetan master. Then, at the age of 40, he became a grateful and humble disciple of a lama at the venerable Zangla monastery. He set about creating a Tibetan dictionary. After 14 years of strenuous work, he produced a corpus of 40,000 words. Later, he wrote a Tibetan grammar. His grammar book is more than a collection of rules: It contains reflections on religious history and dialogues for everyday use.

When he had supplemented his linguistic knowledge with Marathi and Bengali, he felt duly steeled for setting out to achieve his real goal, a study of the origins of the Hungarians.

Fate decided otherwise. He contracted yellow fever, which killed him on April 11, 1842.

Csoma reveals hardly anything about himself in his laconic notes. But his personality and versatile knowledge stirred creative imaginations. Our great storyteller, Mór Jókai, recalls him in the

---

45. From his letter (Dec. 1820, Tehran) to the Protectors of the College of Nagyenyed, where he had studied. Today: Colegiul Național Bethlen din Aiud.

figure of Pál Barkó, a hero of the novel *And Yet It Moves* (1872).

In the book, the president (doctissime) of a boarding school in Debrecen, Ézsaiás Járai, tries to make a student, who is suspected of editing *The Csittvár Chronicle,* talk:

> "Did you promise not to betray each other?"
> Barkó replies with stolid calm:
> "Vermi sözündü geçen, kendi canındı geçen."[46]
> "...That is a Turkish saying. It means, 'Whoever gives up his promise, gives up his soul.' ...Confess your sin honestly in order to free yourself. ...'"
> "Ankeh az daste mardomaan gorikht, sarash dar jazayeh hall avikht."[47]
> "...That is a Persian saying that means, 'The one who avoids a human hand has just sentenced himself to death.' ...Do confess everything now, return from the way of the wicked, and let all be forgiven after that."
> Thereupon Barkó gave the following answer:
> "Teviz birle beklik töride oturmaktin; sever birle chikailik tozida jatmak jekdir!"[48]
> "...Your proverb in Tatar means, 'It is more worthwhile lying in the dust of poverty with a friend than glittering on the throne of power with an enemy.' It proves your dogged obstinacy. Therefore I will not ask you anything else. Recedas, go to the back of the class!"
> And the doctissime indeed made no further inquiries, as he was afraid that the worthless lad would reply to the fourth question in Sanskrit.

Csoma did not consider himself a scholar, only "a humble

---

46. In the novel it is *"Vermis szözündin gecsen, kendi dsánindin gecsen."*
47. In the novel it is *"An ki ezdeszti merdumán gurikht, szeres der dsezai Hakk avikht."*
48. In the novel it is *"Teviz birle beklik töride oturmaktin;—Szever birle csikailik tozida jatmak jekdir!"* Whether the language is Tatar is disputed.

student who wished to see various countries in Asia and learn their languages in the hope that the world would recognize the value of his knowledge."

Rasmus Christian Rask (1787–1832)

I present the Danish philologist Rask after his contemporary, Sándor Kőrösi Csoma, for the sake of sad contrast.

The accomplishments of Csoma were met with indifference by the ruling circles of the country. To support him, the editorial board of the journal *Academic Collection* appealed to the public for donations. Out of the generosity of 11 counties, as well as Professor Hutter of Szombathely and Antal Egyed, parish priest of Paks, 2878 florins and 12 pennies were raised, but this sum probably did not even reach the hands of Csoma.

On the other hand, Rask, the assistant librarian of the University of Copenhagen, had so much money allotted to him by the King via the Treasury that he was able to study the language of Iceland in that country for 10 years. It was Rask who proved that the Icelandic language is related to the others in Europe, and first of all to Latin and Greek. He traveled through Tartary, Persia, India, and Ceylon at public expense, where he located Pali, Zend, Persian, and Sinhalese manuscripts for collections in Copenhagen. This eminent botanist died young, before age 45. He spoke 35 languages; wrote Spanish, Frisian, and Italian grammars for his compatriots; and was the first to write the lines of the *Edda,* Iceland's heroic epic from the Middle Ages.

Heinrich Schliemann (1822–1890)[49]

Vultus fortunae variatur imagine lunae:
crescit, decrescit, constans persistere nescit.

(The course of Fortune changes like the moon:
It grows and shrinks, and knows not how to
stay the same.)

It was on October 3, 1854, in a decisive hour of his adventurous life, that Schliemann caught sight of this inscription while taking a glance at the tower of the Green Gate from the window of his lodgings in Königsberg. By that time, the vagaries of his fate had thrust him into the depths and raised him to the heights countless times.

Schliemann was a country lad who was susceptible to legends and who fell into reveries thinking of ancient tales. An outstanding student at Neustrelitz high school, he had to quit after two years for lack of money. He earned his living for almost six years as an apprentice at small grocery stores. Maybe he would have spent all his life among barrels of herring and sacks of potatoes if he had not suffered a lung hemorrhage caused by lifting a heavy cask. The injury made him unfit for the job. He obtained a position as a cabin-boy on a brig bound for Venezuela, but the *Dorothea* was shipwrecked by a storm near the Dutch shore. He paid his way to Amsterdam with donations from friends. Learning to "write legibly...after 20 lessons from the famous calligraphist," he found employment in an office. He applied himself to studying languages with all his might.

---

49. All references to Schliemann are from his autobiography (1881) unless otherwise noted.

He devised a method to strengthen his bad memory. One should "read a great deal aloud, without making a translation, taking a lesson every day, constantly writing essays upon subjects of interest, correcting these under the supervision of a teacher, learning them by heart, and repeating in the next lesson what was corrected...the previous day." [Furthermore,] "In order to acquire good pronunciation quickly, I went twice every Sunday to the English church, and repeated to myself in a low voice every word of the clergyman's sermon. I never went on my errands, even in the rain, without having my book in my hand and learning something by heart, and I never waited at the post-office without reading. By such methods I gradually strengthened my memory, and in three months' time found no difficulty in reciting from memory...each day's lesson, word by word, 20 printed pages, after having read them over three times attentively." That was how he committed to memory Goldsmith's *Vicar of Wakefield* and Scott's *Ivanhoe*.

"From over-excitement I slept but little and employed my sleepless hours...going over in my mind what I had read the preceding evening...Thus I succeeded in acquiring in half a year a thorough knowledge of the English language."

With this method, he acquired French, also in six months. This time he learned Fénelon's *Les Aventures de Télémaque* and Bernardin de Saint-Pierre's *Paul et Virginie* by heart. "This unremitting study had in the course of a single year strengthened my memory to such a degree that the study of Dutch, Spanish, Italian, and Portuguese appeared very easy, and it did not take me more than six weeks to write and speak each of these languages fluently."

At the age of 22, he managed to obtain a position as correspondent and bookkeeper at a company in Amsterdam. He thought a knowledge of Russian would be necessary to advance. However, in Holland only the vice-consul in the capital knew this language, and he did not consent to give Schliemann lessons. So Schliemann could do nothing but learn the letters and their pronunciation from a grammar, and the words from the Russian version of *Télémaque* by Fénelon. Then, following his usual method, he wrote short stories and learned them by heart. However, it occurred to him that he could make more progress if he had someone to listen to what he had learned: "I hired a poor Jew for four francs a week, who had to come every evening for two hours to listen to my Russian recitations, of which he did not understand a syllable." He was forced to change his lodgings twice, as his neighbors were bothered by the loud recitations.

Fortune's face sometimes darkened, sometimes lit up again over him. His company sent him to Moscow to sell indigo; his operations were so successful that at the age of 25 he was "inscribed in the Guild as a wholesale merchant." However, he was compelled to put his studies aside, and it was not until seven years later that he found it possible to acquire Swedish and Polish.

During the Crimean War, he prepared to go to Memel [then Prussia, now Lithuania] to receive a shipment of 150,000 thalers' worth of indigo from what is now Germany. He passed through Königsberg, and that was where he glimpsed the "ominous inscription" quoted at the beginning of the chapter. Indeed, rumor had it that Memel had been consumed on the previous day by a fearful conflagration. Schliemann learned later that his merchandise had been removed from the massive warehouses of the city and safely housed in a wooden barrack.

He traveled to America in 1850 to search for his brother Ludwig, who had emigrated to California. Heinrich arrived too late: His brother was dead. However, California became a state while he was there. Like everyone else who resided there on that day, he became a naturalized American citizen.

In 1868,[50] the Turks accused him of collecting confidential data with his drawings and surveys for the English, and they banished him from one of his most promising excavation sites.

In 1874, he got into trouble again with the Turks. They wanted a bigger share of the artifacts he had excavated. They made him stop his work again; he had to wait more than two years until he received the firman (edict) that let him continue.

"Like the face of the moon in the sky," fortune and misfortune alternated in Schliemann's commercial activity, and then in his archaeological work as well. Neither of these belong in the framework of my book; I would like to retell only one part of his biography, about his learning the Greek language:

> My wish to learn Greek had always been great, but before the Crimean war I did not venture upon its study, for I was afraid that this language would exercise too great a fascination over me and estrange me from my commercial business, and during the [Crimean] war I was so overwhelmed with work that I could not even read the newspapers, far less a book. When, however, in January 1856, the first tidings of peace reached St. Petersburg, I was no longer able to restrain my desire to learn Greek, and at once I set vigorously to work...I again faithfully followed my old method, but in order to acquire quickly the Greek vocabulary, which seemed to me far more difficult even than the Russian, I procured a Modern Greek

---

50. The date given in the Hungarian edition of this book is 1862, but other sources mention 1868 as the date of Schliemann's first visit to Turkey.

translation of *Paul et Virginie*. I read it through, comparing every word with its equivalent in the French original. When I had finished this task, I knew at least one-half the Greek words the book contained and, after repeating the operation, I knew them all, or nearly so, without having lost a single minute by being obliged to use a dictionary. In this manner it did not take me more than six weeks to master the difficulties of Modern Greek, and I next applied myself to the ancient language, of which in three months I learned enough to understand some of the ancient authors, and especially Homer, whom I read and re-read with the most lively enthusiasm...

Of the Greek grammar, I learned only the declensions and the verbs, but I never wasted my precious time in studying its rules; I saw that boys, after being troubled and tormented for eight years or more in schools with the tedious rules of grammar, can nevertheless none of them write a letter in Ancient Greek without making hundreds of atrocious blunders. I thought the method pursued by the schoolmasters must be altogether wrong, and that a thorough knowledge of the Greek grammar could be obtained only by practice—that is to say, by the attentive reading of the prose classics, and by committing choice pieces of them to memory. Following this very simple method, I learned Ancient Greek as I would have learned a living language. I can write in it with the greatest fluency on any subject I am acquainted with and can never forget it...

It is a cruel injustice to inflict for years upon an unhappy pupil a language of which, when he leaves college, as a general rule, he knows hardly more than when he first began to learn it...

In the year 1858 I thought I had money enough and wished to retire from commercial pursuits. I traveled in Sweden, Denmark, Germany [Prussia], Italy, and Egypt, where I sailed up the Nile as far as the Second Cataracts...I visited Petra and traversed the whole of Syria, and in this manner had abundant opportunity to acquire a practical knowledge of Arabic, the deeper study of which I continued afterward in St. Petersburg.

The treasure unearthed by Schliemann resides today in the museums of Athens, London, and Berlin. Few of the hundreds of thousands of visitors realize that bringing this cultural heritage to the surface required a combination of a childlike naive belief and manly perseverance that borders on the miraculous.

It is also a miracle that Schliemann, who completed only two years of high school, received the highest academic rank of the age. He attached a long dissertation in Ancient Greek to his first travel description, for which the University of Rostock in his native Mecklenburg honored him with a Doctor of Philosophy degree.

Ármin Vámbéry (1832–1913)[51]

Ármin Vámbéry was "a traveler of Central Asia, world-famous Orientalist, university professor, [and] excellent authority on Turkish philology," as the encyclopedia says about him.[52] His marvelous willpower is depicted in novels and adventure films. Lame, poor, literally leaning on a beggar's stick, he wandered through the vast desert of Karakum [Turkmenistan]. The truths and errors of his linguistic ideas are the subject of philological studies. Readers of his travelogues are spellbound by the fresh and colorful depictions of regions and people.

In accordance with the topic of my book, we are interested in how he was able to acquire a dozen languages by age 18. He was able to polish some of them later to such a degree that their perfection nearly jeopardized his credibility. Some insisted in London that whoever speaks Persian and Turkish so impeccably and

---

51. All references to Vámbéry are from his autobiography (1904) unless otherwise noted.
52. The encyclopedia Lomb refers to could not be located.

without any accent can be only a disguised Asian, not a European.

I would like to cite the excerpts of his autobiography that concern his language studies.

First, however, I must remark that inhabitants of some areas have better than average opportunities for conquering the country of Polyglottia. For example, a native of Transylvania, who hears Hungarian at home, Romanian at school, and German from his Saxon friends, will set about learning other tongues with the *awareness*—even if not the knowledge—of three languages. Jews, after the Diaspora scattered them in the world, have always had a high percentage of multilinguals. Let us recall three eminent Hungarian Orientalists: Ármin Vámbéry, Ignác Goldziher, and Ignác Kúnos. Jewish religious traditions prescribed that a five- or six-year-old son should become acquainted with—apart from the local tongue—Hebrew. Although this exposure is usually limited to learning another kind of alphabet and reading the holy scriptures, Jews' eyes are opened up to the multilingualism of the world. Based on the reports of my subjects, this kind of experience is a deciding factor in success at language acquisition.

I would like to present one fact in support of my conviction that Jews do not owe their well-known polyglottism to some special talent for languages. This duality ceased to exist in Israel: The language of religion and the language of the state merged. The foreign language skills of those born there are not higher than the skills of youth of similar social class in other countries.

Although Vámbéry learned long passages from the Book of Isaiah and the Book of Jeremiah by the age of eight, in terms of secular studies he did not exceed basic literacy in Hungarian and German. It was only thanks to the ambition and cleverness of his mother that he learned elementary Latin, geography, and natural history in his Protestant primary school.

At the school in Dunajská Streda, he excelled at languages. At the exam, in front of an illustrious guest, György Bartal, a knight of the Golden Spur, he recited a long Latin poem by heart. Then, with the encouragement of his teacher, he recited it backwards as well.

In Dunajská Streda, as well as in Svätý Jur, where he attended the Piarist high school, Vámbéry often went hungry and suffered from ethnic intolerance. He went to Bratislava, where he was able to pay for his lodgings and daily bread by private tutoring and manual labor. As he wrote in his autobiography, *The Story of My Struggles,* his consolation for his miserable fate was that he could occupy his youthful mind in his own way. "I turned my attention to the acquisition of languages because of the ease with which I could use Latin for general conversation, and because when I began my studies I knew four languages (Hungarian, German, Slavic, and Hebrew)." He obtained a French textbook that showed proper pronunciation, but unfortunately these markings were in German. "It was, of course, a miserable pronunciation, but...I was, after a few weeks' time, full of hope that I should soon be able to speak French. When alone, I used to make up sentences or carry on a conversation with myself, or I read the most trivial things, declaiming them with great pathos...I conversed in French without restraint...It became such a mania with me that I addressed everyone in French—peasants, tradespeople, merchants, Slavs, Germans, and Hungarians. It was all the same to me, and great was my delight if they stared at me and admired me for my learning."

In the sixth grade he changed schools, entering the Protestant Lyceum. But the calendar showed 1849; the suppressed revolution and war of independence put an end to the hopes of Hungary and to his schooling as well. Vámbéry could not even procure a certificate to testify that he passed his exams: He didn't have 16 florins.

He traveled to Pest, where the Austrian reign of terror that followed the struggle for [Hungarian] independence had left its sorrowful mark upon the city and the people. He tried to find a job as a tutor. "I could read German, French, and Italian fairly well without the help of a dictionary; Hebrew and Latin I knew slightly, and of course I could speak and write my two native tongues, Hungarian and Slavic. On the strength of these accomplishments I had the audacity to advertise myself as professor of seven languages." A country merchant, who came to Pest for the St. Joseph fair, hired Vámbéry as a private tutor in Kutjevo, Slavonia (Croatia). At last he is given a comfortable room and good food; he can devote himself to the Turkish language and Oriental studies. Unfortunately, he falls in love with a beautiful young daughter of the family and tries to win her heart by reading her the sonnets of Petrarch. He tries to substitute the daughter's name in the poem for that of the poet's love. Alas, "Emília" is one syllable longer than "Laura," so his objective is thwarted by meter. He finds comfort in learning more languages.

"I began to build my airy castles for the future. To the seven languages I knew I had gradually added Spanish, Danish, and Swedish, all of which I learned in a comparatively short time, sufficiently at any rate to appreciate the literary productions of these various countries...At the same time I made steady progress in Turkish, for in my passion for learning, strengthened by an ever-growing power of retention, I had indeed accomplished wonders. Whenever in my readings I came upon words...that I did not know, I wrote them down and committed them to memory, at first from 10 to 20 per day...to as many as 80 or even 100." Hence, "In this consciousness I boldly faced the future with all the disappointments that possibly might await me in the thorny path of life, whether owing to accident or to my own fault," as he recounts in his autobiography.

This happy state of affairs came to an end when the parents noticed the burgeoning romance and found it better to dismiss the amorous tutor. He had no choice but to bid farewell to the scenic Croatian mountains and return to the capital [Pest].

In the meantime he learned the "South-Slavonic" language as well. He thought he could work at the Ministry of Foreign Affairs of the Monarchy. He traveled to Vienna and applied for a position as an interpreter, but to no avail. He returned to Pest and managed to find a job as a language tutor: He taught Hungarian to the offspring of the slowly developing Hungarian citizenry, who were not quite familiar with this tongue after years of German being the language of the ruling class.

"During this interval of my professional duties I devoted daily 10 or 12 hours assiduously to linguistic studies. To the Romanic and Germanic languages I had added the study of the Slavonic dialects. The Slovak dialect I had learned conversationally at St. George[53] and Zsámbokrét;[54] Illyric [Croatian] at Kutjevo; I had also studied the literatures of these languages. I now applied myself to learn Russian, which of course was a comparatively easy matter, and I reveled in the works of Pushkin, Lermontov, Batyushkov, Derzhavin, and other northern writers."

In Pest he found the milieu that has provided home and

53. Szentgyörgy.
54. Today: Žabokreky in Slovakia.

school for so many predecessors and successors in every part of the world: the university library.

The single-story building was open for only two hours in the morning, and from two to six in the afternoon, but he received permission to spend the break hours there, perusing the Koran and the Turkish–Latin dictionary.

Yet he left the capital. Mr. Mayer, an agent for teachers and a regular at the Café Orczy, found him a job with a wealthy family in Kecskemét.[55] Thanks to a professor at the Protestant Lyceum of Kecskemét, he obtained Arabic books. He wrote, "Thus I was able, assisted by my knowledge of Hebrew, to make rapid progress in the second Semitic language. ...The strange characters, the difficulty of learning to read, and the want of dictionaries, which were too expensive for me to buy, were terrible obstacles in my way; often I was almost driven to distraction, and the hours spent in the shady little Protestant churchyard of Kecskemét, where I loved to linger near the grave of two lovers, will ever remain in my memory."

At the age of 73 he began writing his life story based on notes he made in Hungarian and letters he wrote in Arabic during his travels. At that time, he was already a world-renowned Orientalist and a friend of Ferenc Deák,[56] Jókai Mór, and Baron Eötvös.[57] He repeatedly visited Turkey, Persia, northern Afghanistan, and Bukhara [Uzbekistan]. His academic papers and travelogues were published in German, English, French, and Hungarian. After much delay and strife, he was awarded a university professorship and Academy membership.

55. A city near the center of Hungary.
56. Hungarian statesman and Minister of Justice (1803–1876).
57. József Baron Eötvös, Hungarian statesman (1813–1871).

Still, in his autobiography he does not shrink from criticizing himself and his learning method.

"I had an immense number of foreign languages in my head. I could say by heart long passages from the *Parnasso Italiano*, Byron, Pushkin, Tegnér, and Saadi. I could speak fluently and write moderately well in several of these languages, yet my learning was absolutely without system or method, and it was not until I had had actual communication with the various nations and had paid the penalty of my many shortcomings and erroneous notions, that I could rejoice in having attained a certain degree of fluency. It is chiefly due to this haste and eagerness to get on that in the course of my later studies I always preferred a wide field of action rather than great depth, and I always set my mind rather on expansion than on penetration."

From Professor Ármin Vámbéry, the world-famous Orientalist, we, his successors and admirers, can learn modesty as well.

Alexander Lenard[58] (1910–1972)

I was not able to interview him, as he has been residing since 1972 in Blumenau, Brazil, under the araucaria trees of his garden. The definitive biography on him is still waiting to be written. It was from his books and Mrs. Antal Szerb's[59] generous help that I could compile the material that establishes his deserved place in the Pantheon of Polyglots. He excelled as a human being, a physician, a musician, an art historian, and finally a linguist. Above all, he excelled as a writer. Since Ferenc Móra,[60] nobody could

---

58.   In the original Hungarian: Sándor Lénard or Lénárd.
59.   The widow of the famed Hungarian writer Antal Szerb (1901–1945).
60.   Noted Hungarian writer (1879–1934).

disassemble the wide spectrum of the Hungarian language into the colors of the rainbow and then again transform it magically into white as he did in his novels *Valley at the End of the World,*[61] *Roman Stories, A Day in the Invisible House,* and other works.

His use of Hungarian is all the more marvelous when we consider that he left Hungary in 1918, at the age of eight. He attended university in Austria. Later, after the Anschluss,[62] he went to Italy as a starving émigré. Italy was not friendly at that time, being under the bloody rule of Mussolini, the Fascist clown.

What languages did he speak? All that he happened to need. He writes about his experiences during the war: "[In Italy] we were listening to the London radio—its broadcast in Danish was not jammed—and in our excited enthusiasm we knew Danish excellently (all at once we grasped the Pentecost miracle of the apostles: We listened to and understood the great events in Icelandic, Romanian, Portuguese, and Luxembourgish)."[63]

In Rome he had neither bread nor home. The shelter of all roofless people, the library, gave refuge to him.

> I was looking for something—a concept—in the large Brockhaus,[64] when someone addressed me:
> "Are you a foreigner?"
> "Yes, I am."
> "Do you happen to speak Dutch?"
> In fact, I didn't speak Dutch, but I spoke German, English, and some Swedish. In addition, my shoes needed new soles...I answered cautiously: "I suppose I know enough for your purposes."

---

61. His English translation was published as *The Valley of the Latin Bear.*
62. The occupation of Austria and annexation into Nazi Germany in 1938.
63. Lenard, *Roman Stories* (1969). All references to Lenard are from this volume unless otherwise noted.
64. A German-language encyclopedia.

"It is luck indeed!...I need a translation from Dutch. It's *Het Evenwichtsbegrip in de economische literatuur* by Keesing."

"I'm afraid my Italian style is not appropriate."

"It's not a problem. I don't want to publish it, just read it. If an expression is too difficult, you can supply it in French or English. All I want to know is what the work contains." Then, with a precision worthy of a professor of economics and financial theory, he added: "I would pay five lire[65] per page."

It was worth knowing Dutch for this amount. From translating just two pages, I could stroll along with dry feet for a month.

"How many pages does it have?"

"Three hundred. But it's not urgent. If you translate a hundred pages in a month and bring it to me..."

Fifteen hundred lire! After all, I spoke Dutch pretty well. And I could find enough dictionaries to help me. I could translate three pages in three hours—then read two or even more...

One of his fellow émigrés—another starving medical expert—hoped that he could earn his bread on a Norwegian fishing vessel. Lenard promised him he would teach him Norwegian. It is just that Lenard had to acquire it first:

"We find a Bible in Norwegian at the British Bible Society, and we try to deduce enough grammar principles from The Book of Revelation by John so that a whale-hunting Hungarian dentist can survive." The friend, about to leave on the fishing boat, offered Lenard a blood pressure meter to survive on. "Give it to me," Lenard said, "I'll pay for it with the irregular verbs." He taught German to a would-be official. The remuneration was a pair of old pants. "The knees were perfect."

After the war, Lenard worked as a physician at the Hungarian

---

65. *Lira* (plural: *lire*): the currency of Italy between 1861 and 2002.

Academy in Rome. Then he emigrated to Brazil in 1951. In 1956, he won the Bach competition sponsored by São Paulo Television. With the prize money he bought a garden and built a house.

In 1968, he was invited to be a professor at the University of Charleston in West Virginia. They expected him to teach not only Latin but also the entire classical philology (including Greek). He acquired Homer's language during the two months of the summer vacation. Subsequently, he taught for four semesters in Charleston.

In the end he returned to the "invisible house" he had built in the valley of Donna Emma,[66] in the middle of the Brazilian jungle. There—as the English-language encyclopedias put it—he healed natives, played Bach on his organ, wrote novels, and studied the classics. He did not translate his books but wrote them separately in Hungarian, Italian, German, and English. He did so "in order that the 'local color' could stand out in each of them," as Mrs. Szerb, his friend faithful to the grave, explained.

He wrote his poems in German. In this language, not considered especially lyric, he could bring out soft and poetic sounds. But he courted his current lady in a way that percolated with linguistic humor. Here is the translation of one of his love poems:

For C.

If you were Tuscan, my darling,
I would study Dante for you,
I would wander across the tercets
until I knew you as he knew Beatrice.

---

66.   Also referred to as "Donna Irma" in the English edition of his novel (*The Valley of the Latin Bear*).

> If you were Chinese, I'd pave the way
> Through the jungle of black characters
> If you were in Spain, I'd ride there
> so as to be your faithful Sancho Panza.
>
> If you were thinking in Greek, I'd seek Xenophon
> with all his unpredictable verbs—
> But you think in English! I already speak it!
> So all I want is: to die for you.[67]

I could not ask Alexander Lenard my obligatory questions. But I know his opinion on world languages. He was an enthusiastic fanatic and inspired re-creator of Latin. He was of the opinion that Latin is not dead but asleep. Indeed, in the middle of the 20th century Latin-language young adult books were published and became bestsellers. Although the first translation in this trend, *Robinson Crusoe* by the Hungarian-born Avellanus, went unnoticed, Maffacini's *Pinoculus,* from the popular *Pinocchio,* ran to six editions in Italy. But the crown belongs to Alexander Lenard.

To win the Anglo-Saxon world over to Latin, he translated A. A. Milne's charming *Winnie-the-Pooh.* This book, just like *The Little Prince* by Antoine de Saint-Exupéry, achieved worldwide success in Latin. *Max and Moritz* became a popular hit too in Lenard's translation, as well as *Bonjour Tristesse* (Françoise Sagan),

---

67. The original: *Für C. // Wärst Du Geliebteste, Toscanerin, / Studierte ich um Dich zu kennen Dante, / Durch die Terzinen wanderte mein Sinn / Bis er Dich gut, wie Beatricen kannte, // Wärst Du Chinesin, bahnte ich den Weg / Durch einen Urwald schwarzer Charaktäre; / Wärst Du in Spanien, ritte ich dahin / Dass ich getreu Dein Sancho Panza wäre, // Dächtest Du griechisch sucht ich Xenophon / Mit allen unberechenbaren Verben—/ Doch Du denkst Englisch! Englisch kann ich schon! / So plan ich eines nur: für Dich zu sterben.*

translated into Latin for adults. He chose this work, published under the title *Tristitia Salve,* because it portrays love—an old theme!—in a modern setting, on the French Riviera. Another reason why he chose the book was because the beautiful lady writer of the novel had scorched the heart of the 50ish translator.

Apart from the Slavic tongues, Lenard "knew all languages." He knew several of them as perfectly as he knew Hungarian.

But when he was asked which one he felt was his real mother tongue, he replied:

"Bach."

What Is the Good
Language Learner Like?

≈

IT STARTED with a letter from Sweden. The letter was to
me and to more than a hundred other linguaphiles around the
world, people who are known in professional circles as having
devoted their lives to learning languages.

The letter was from a professor at the university there, Dr.
Karin Kitzing. She pointed out that the question of language
learning had been examined in the academic literature rather one-
sidedly. Numerous books and articles had discussed the problems
of teachers, methods, and results, but few had investigated what
takes place in the *learner* when he or she becomes familiar with a
new language. Speaking in terms of computer science: We already
know the problem of input and output, but there is still a lot to
be known about the processing of data.

This omission is understandable. Education is mostly limited
to schools, and educators hardly ever study how pupils learn.

That was why Dr. Kitzing and Lund University resolved to
contact polyglots in Europe (and some countries outside of Europe)

to let them talk about themselves and how they learn languages. I represented Hungary on their list.

In all, 88 [actually 76] replies arrived from 22 countries. The respondents had 19 native languages. The youngest was 15 years old; the oldest, 72. Most of them had grown up in a monolingual environment; only 28% claimed to be natively bilingual.

There were native speakers of Swedish, Polish, Finnish, French, Norwegian, Persian, Hungarian, Russian, Tunisian Arabic, Schwyzerdütsch (Swiss German), and Luxembourgish. However, there were only three native English speakers. This small number is surprising if we consider that around 400 million people call English their first language. It is true that Britain is an island, and the United States even more so metaphorically, but native English speakers have an advantage in learning foreign languages compared to others. If English speakers wish to learn French, Italian, Spanish, or Portuguese, they are already familiar with more than half of those languages' vocabularies. If they choose German, Dutch, or Swedish, they're familiar with more than a quarter of the words. According to Frederick Bodmer, author of *The Loom of Language*, Anglo-Americans should be able to learn at least some foreign languages reasonably well by virtue of birthplace.

Yet they do not. There are two reasons. One is lack of motivation—other speakers bend over backwards to make themselves understood in English. But English speakers' low ranking on the list is also explained by a common trait: their inclination for understatement.

A genuine English gentleman will not claim to be the best at anything, not even the mastery of languages!

I hope the reader will forgive me if I quote an old joke that, if tinkered with slightly, can be recast as a linguistic joke. First, I present the original joke:

If a diplomat says "Yes," he means "Maybe." If a diplomat says "Maybe," he means "No." If a diplomat says "No," he is no diplomat. If a lady says "No," she means "Maybe." If a lady says "Maybe," she means "Yes." If a lady says "Yes," she is no lady.

Here is the linguistic version of the joke:

If an Englishman says that he doesn't speak a foreign language "at all," he speaks it a little. If he says "a little," he speaks it perfectly. If he says "perfectly," he is no Englishman. On the other hand, if a Hungarian says that he speaks a language "perfectly," he speaks it a little; if he says "a little," he doesn't speak it at all; and if he says "not at all," he is not a Hungarian.

Among those who sent "interesting answers" to Dr. Kitzing's questionnaire, not one claimed English as his or her native tongue.

I know about the English respondents because I went to Sweden, and Dr. Kitzing and I selected the answers that contained original ideas. It was only through long correspondence and some connections that I got three native speakers of English to admit their polyglottism and answer my questions.

The aim of the Swedish questionnaire was to construct a model of the "Good Language Learner." The method was self-assessment. The polyglots were asked to grade their own skills, quite like at school. The grade 5 meant A (high), and 1 meant F (low).

I thought that, of the skills, the respondents would grade themselves most highly in memory. I was wrong: Only one quarter of the respondents gave themselves an A (5) for memory.

Of the respondents, 51% believed that they deserved an A for the imitation of speech sounds, while only 31% believed they deserved an A for the imitation of intonation.

The second question was, What gifts do you consider decisive for successful language learning? For example, how much of a role do you attribute to language aptitude? A total of 4% deemed it "less important"; 5% said "unimportant." More important than linguistic skills was motivation; 92% asserted that there is no effective language learning without motivation. Some ranked it most important, others as second-most important. No one called it unimportant.

Another question asked about the personal motivation of each respondent. For 53%, the motivation was being interested in people; for 51%, it was to be a part of society. Relatively few people referred to usefulness at work as being a motivator, and only 33% mentioned an attraction to linguistics as a driver.

Two-thirds of the respondents stated that self-esteem was an important or very important factor in successful language learning. The only factors that achieved a better grade were empathy and perception of patterns.

These two concepts may require some explanation. By perception of patterns we mean the skill in finding patterns typical of a foreign language; some learners recognize these patterns and dare to apply the rules that enable them to form words and create sentences. This skill is called field independence in English. The only reason I write it here is that it sounds so nicely pompous.

Empathy is a psychological concept, a capacity to recognize the feelings of others. Only one respondent dared to confess that he or she did very poorly in this field. If I can count on your discretion, I will disclose that I was this solitary person.

What did the respondents consider more important to succeed quickly: formal learning or permanent exposure to the language?

Learning received an A or B from only 66%; exposure received an A or B from 95%.

Unfortunately.[68]

In practice, relationships are not easy to establish and not easy to maintain. Apart from your teachers, whom can you expect to be at your disposal and to endure your stuttering attempts with resignation (or maybe even correct them)? Can you expect your foreign acquaintances to always be patient—especially if you can already communicate with them in a common language?

Apart from a conversation with oneself, which I advocate frequently (and which I named *autologue* because neither *monologue* nor *dialogue* covers the concept), there is one situation I find suitable for conversation: a relative, friend, or acquaintance visiting you from abroad who—out of gratitude for showing him around—will allow you to practice with him. He might even warn you—possibly tactfully—of your mistakes.

By the way, it is not only a personal but also a national trait that determines how much someone tolerates the incorrect, broken speech of non-natives. A phlegmatic Englishman will not object at all. He has gotten used to the fact that even his compatriots speak differently, depending on their residence and social class, let alone speakers of American or Canadian English and the "faulty" pronunciation of job seekers who arrive from the former British colonies.

The French are intolerant. If people are well-mannered, they will only grumble to themselves; if they are uneducated, they will express their dislike with a grimace. I think it is their pride that makes them aggressive. They haven't yet gotten used to the fact

---

68. The following seven paragraphs appear in slightly different form in Lomb's first book, *Polyglot: How I Learn Languages*, pp. 64–5.

that French, once a means of communication between emperors and ambassadors, is now tumbling from the lips of low-budget tourists.

I see another difficulty in practicing a language with others. An uninteresting partner is uninteresting in a foreign language as well.

I have written about how much I suffered in Japan because everyone wanted to practice English with me, and I couldn't get answers in Japanese to my questions in Japanese. In the end, someone took pity on me and recommended a certain Mr. Matsumoto, who understood my sorrow and showed willingness to converse with me in Japanese in the afternoons.

Mr. Matsumoto proved to be a Buddhist monk. He was indeed ready to converse in Japanese, but unfortunately his only topic was Buddhism; specifically, that 11 of its 12 branches held completely false views. Only the branch that he followed was the true one. While he was explaining to me what the sole correct interpretation of the Lotus Sutra was for the third hour, I slipped away.

Returning to the Swedish survey: My colleagues at Lund University were kind enough to make the results available to me. They even authorized me to publish the data they did not intend to use in their articles. This was data that they considered mathematically inexpressible, statistically indeterminate, or unquantifiable.

Regarding today's publications in psychology, pedagogy, philosophy, linguistics, etc., I often have the impression that the writers create their articles first, and then they insert the quantification: the probability coefficient, the correlation significance, and the results of the regression analysis. They do so because no academic worthy of the name will submit anything for publication without these numbers.

Data from psychological measurements—psychometrics—are interesting. But someone who examines only the body of a butterfly stuck to a board with a pin will never be able to understand the notion of the fluttering of its wings!

My Swedish partners considered the answers to the last item on the survey to be statistically indeterminate. The item was not a question but a request: Describe the features of the Good Language Learner.

My partners made the material available to me with the comment that it wouldn't get me very far. The Good Language Learner has no specific traits, they said.

They were wrong. The answers unraveled the intellectual and personality traits of this sort of person as unambiguously as a skillfully drawn police profile.

The Good Language Learner is:
- Curious
- Playful
- Optimistic
- Talkative, with a lively temperament
- A "key-seeker," who hunts for connections with pleasure
- Brave enough to apply what he or she has studied recently
- "Of a watchful ear"
- Not vain and not conceited
- Ready to be checked and to check herself
- Flexible as to limits of personality
- Fond of books

- Open to other people and cultures
- Inclined to (play)act
- Happy to solve puzzles and untie knots
- Tolerant of uncertainty

Many respondents expressed that the Good Language Learner is not afraid of being laughed at or taken for a jackass. "I learned the most," someone wrote, "by noticing if my partner didn't understand what I said."

A common statement that was especially close to my heart was, "Play is a good way to learn something." I have always attributed my own results to the fact that I never saw learning as a job; I always managed to transform it into amusement or fun.

I have always played with languages.

I confess that I never liked taking lessons. I don't like learning from course books, either; I usually use them to check my knowledge rather than to acquire it. I generally learn from books that professionally interest me or from literary works that simply entertain me.

Of course, this kind of knowledge, acquired from books and radio performances, is random, and there is a higher risk of gaps emerging with this method. However, the ever-so-amusing minutes are likely to lengthen into hours, during which time the gaps can be filled, and the salient points recognized as such.

None of the polyglots mentioned three good qualities that are indispensable if one wants to succeed: diligence, persistence, and self-discipline. Obviously these virtues are required not only for learning languages but for all activities. That is why I have the quite controversial opinion that the result does not derive from some mystical talent for languages, but from general good qualities and a special motivation.

Naturally, we must admit that the listed faculties—such as a sensitive ear and an inclination to act—are more necessary for a linguaphile than for, say, a dentist or a nuclear scientist. But I maintain that the so-called talent has numerous components, and these components often make up for any lacking skills.

A widely acclaimed colleague drew me aside not long ago and, blushing, asked me to tell her what on earth the dative case was. "I really ought to know it," she said, "as I have been living by simultaneous interpreting for years."

Here I could refer to a literary translator who translated texts into 10 languages with unparalleled perfection. He spoke each of them—but with a Hungarian accent that forced the listener to guess which language he was speaking.

Back to the qualities of the Good Language Learner: I believe the list omits one feature that I cannot imagine a genuine linguaphile would lack. I think a linguaphile is characterized by his or her view that the *form* of the message is as important as its *content*. In fact a linguaphile reacts to a form—which is but a means of communication—more intensely than the content it carries.

The world of a linguaphile is a world turned upside down. It is as if the real building were not the beautiful palace on the bank of the Danube, but its reflection rolling on the waves of the river. They feel more familiar in this reflected medium than in the real one.

Fortunately, we are in good company. Cicero once described poets as people who pay more attention to sounds than to things.

I saw a beautiful painting by Filippo Lippi in Italy. He portrayed the Christ child in the midst of six angels. For the edification of the beholders, Lippi painted the names of the angels as well:

Prudenza (Prudence), Fortezza (Fortitude), Pazienza (Patience), Fede (Faith), Speranza (Hope), and Verginità (Virginity).

Even if the last angel cannot be regarded as an absolute prerequisite for successful language learning, the others are necessary, without exception, to proceed with learning at a good pace.

First of all is patience.

In the very first period of our lives, all we do is acquire a language—under the best possible circumstances. Yet we need five or six years to reach the level required by primary school. What if a three-year-old lost her patience at not yet being able to roll her r's properly and simply dropped out of her native language course?

From the point of view of a new language, all of us are infants. Patience is a prerequisite for successful language learning just as patience is a prerequisite for successful fishing. Patience is more often mentioned in connection with angling: You have to crouch by the waterside for hours until a pike or a catfish takes the hook. Yet fishing is apt; its tool is a net. We, language learners, plunge this net into the sea of words. When we start pulling it out, the words and the rules that link the words into sentences lift each other into our minds as the intertwined little strands of a net do with the catch.

When you start speaking a language that you have not used for a long time or know poorly, the wheels of your mind turn slowly and grind. Then you get the hang of it; what's more, you get wings. The net of your memory gradually emerges from the deep water. Words you thought were forgotten come to the surface; a rule lurking somewhere in your mind transforms them into correct sentences.

Though I do not want to refer again to the fabric or context that holds words together—I can hear people mocking me as "Kati Kontext" behind my back—there is one situation that calls for context. That situation is the language-learning skills of the elderly.

A child's memory is automatic; an adult's is logical. A preschool child can learn nonsense ditties without difficulty. An adult will remember only what can be included in the train of his or her thoughts. Tracking consolidates more and more with age; it stiffens beyond age 50 or 60. Whatever cannot have a place in the chain of logic—above all, names of people, streets, and cities—will be hard to memorize and difficult to recall. The diminished memory of names is a well-known fact and the topic of many jokes.

We know that eyes become far-sighted in later life: They will see distant images better and closer ones worse. Seldom do we hear about intellectual farsightedness, however. Yet it exists. We see the big picture, but the details within the picture are blurred. The older mind cannot recall particulars, such as names, that are not connected logically to the rest of our field of vision. There is no association to help bridge the gaps.

One of my most multilingual interviewees admitted that sometimes he consciously remembers only the first and the last letter of the names of people, places, or foreign terms with which he is not entirely familiar. That is, he remembers the perspective, the framework. It rings a bell!

For example, you think nostalgically of the erstwhile café where they served, in addition to coffee, a great variety of daily and weekly newspapers from around the world. The whole furniture of the place appears in your mind's eye; it even dawns on you that its name had a "b," a "u," and an "i," but you cannot recall it. You get annoyed; annoyance empties your mind and tightens your recall even more. Then, when the stress is gone (because you have resigned yourself to forgetting the name), you suddenly cry out triumphantly, "Bucsinszky!"

Why does this diminishing of the memory of names happen—usually to those over 50—even to people who can otherwise express themselves smoothly and precisely (even in the stressful environment of simultaneous interpreting)? It is because the little knots of logic become more tightly connected to each other with age. Thus the role of association increases. The more years you have lived, the more experiences and memories you have piled up in your mind. They ask to speak when a train of thought is formed, and they displace designations that are not yet logically justified and do not have relevant meaning to you. When old people tell anecdotes endlessly and bore young people, the teeming associations come to the surface.

Language is a net of connections in every age, even if not as stiffened as with the elderly. It gives rise to conclusions pertaining to the Good Language Learner. Whoever wants to acquire words and rules in an isolated form, out of connections, will memorize them poorly. The Good Language Learner will memorize groups of words ("I put up resistance," "you play a part," "s/he makes an impression"). Linked words, like little knots of a net, help each other come to the surface.

I can only hope that the Angel of Patience is still hovering above the heads of my Dear Readers and will make you forgive me for this lengthy detour.

A Report on an Imaginary
Round Table of Polyglots

≈

I COULD NOT have brought my distinguished interviewees together even if Comecon, the European Economic Community, or a major international organization had supported me and
organized a conference on language learning. I dared not, even in
my mind, apply to the United Nations Security Council for the
funds to organize such a gathering. There was nothing I could do
but seat my proud polyglots at an imaginary round table.

(Let the interpreter within me explain why the round-table
format has become more and more popular with conference
organizers: No guest's sensitive ego is threatened. The idea may
have originated with the legendary King Arthur, who thereby
ensured that each knight felt that his noble mission was equally
important.)

At my round table conference, no ego conflicts arose.
Unfortunately, there were no positive interpersonal interactions
either. There was no exchange of views in the lobbies, sometimes
overshadowing official speeches; no introductions and socializing

during the long-awaited coffee breaks; no business lunches and evening receptions; no horse shows at Bugacpuszta;[69] and no wine tastings in the Tokaj cellars.[70] More than that, I could not organize a sightseeing-cum-fashion show for the accompanying wives or partners. But at least I did not have to be worried about delegates from the East being diverted from attending the conferences by the glitter of Váci Street shop windows, or those from the West distracted by the in-depth exploration of women's issues in Hungary.

I missed the excited whisper of interpreters in the booths: "Oh my goodness, this one is speaking about something completely different from the title of his lecture." But no interpreters were necessary; the participants had six or eight languages in common.

The first agenda item of conferences did not take place: electing a chairperson. The usual ceremony was omitted. The representative of the host country rose to speak and announced that he or she proposed Mr. or Ms. X for this post. Were there any counter-proposals?

There were no counter-proposals; the newly elected chairperson thanked attendees for the completely unexpected and surprising honor in a well-turned little speech, the text of which had already been distributed among the interpreters, copied, and translated into every language at the conference.

These solemn minutes will now be lacking. Turning my back

---

69. Also known as *Bugac:* a village and exhibition on the Great Hungarian Plain, noted for the *puszta* (vast area of plains), its specially protected native juniper grove, its traditional gray cattle breed, and its nomadic horse culture.

70. *Tokaji* is the most famous wine brand of Hungary, deriving from the Tokaj-Hegyalja wine region in northeastern Hungary.

on the most basic rules of democracy, I unanimously proclaimed myself chair. A dual task weighed on my shoulders, though. On the one hand, I had to voice my own views in connection with the various items; on the other hand, I had to ensure strict compliance with the agenda.

How did I handle this dual load? I abused my power as chair and never rang the bell on myself, and I did not call myself to order even when I had long exceeded the time allowed for individual contributions.

I did not provide a list of participants. I introduced them one by one instead. After the introductions, they will be referred to by their surnames. I hereby apologize for omitting any patronymics, academic titles, and forms of address, such as Monsignor, Monsieur, Mister, or Herr.

Introducing the participants

I wanted to present a more well-rounded picture of the inhabitants of Polyglottia than what was provided by the Swedish survey. Through some fairly long correspondence with people in the U.K., I managed to find three interviewees who admitted their multilingualism and were ready to introduce themselves to my readers. I thank the Institute of Linguists, which helped me meet these interviewees.

I had another, bolder plan as well. I have long marveled at John Paul II's linguistic virtuosity on the radio: e.g., his Christmas greetings in many languages, and his Russian with Soviet interviewers. I steeled myself to the point where I had enough courage to make an immodest move: I asked the Vatican for an interview with the pope about his multilingualism.

The most reverend rector of the Hungarian Papal Institute in Rome was willing to mediate on my behalf. After a few weeks' waiting, I was informed that my request—due to the pope's being extremely occupied—could not be fulfilled. The letter in which the Secretariat of State of the Vatican communicated this simple "no" to the intermediary of the request is such an instructive document of diplomatic politeness that it is worth publishing here. For a reason unknown to me, its sender bestowed upon me a title and rank that is undeserved and was never claimed.

Most Reverend Sir,

In your letter dated the 8th of this current March, you forwarded to the Secretariat of State a message by Prof. Katherina Lomb, who will soon arrive in Rome. The above-mentioned Lecturer has expressed the wish to be able to meet the Holy Father, or at least to receive His substantive answers to a questionnaire pertaining to the knowledge and faculty of acquiring foreign languages.

His Holiness appreciates the obliging idea and asks you to forward to the writer, along with a word of exhortation, the expression of His gratitude for the manifestation of respect, gladly sending His blessings to the kind lady.

As far as the subject of the request is concerned, I have been charged to notify you that the issue has been examined with the necessary attention, but despite all good will, it does not seem feasible.

Asking you to communicate the message in whatever form you find opportune with the intermediary, I thank you for the cooperation and take this opportunity to greet you with respect.

Yours faithfully,

Colasuonno

Despite this rejection, I was able to conduct an interview in the Congregatio de Disciplina Sacramentorum (the Congregation for the Discipline of the Sacraments),[71] at Piazza Pio XII, with a multifaceted Vatican diplomat respected for his linguistic mastery. Needless to say, he was of Hungarian descent.

Let me now introduce those who did consent to an interview and/or replied to my questions. First is Monsignor Arcivescovo Dottore Luigi Kada, Archbishop Lajos Kada.

He answered my questions in Hungarian. Although he had not been to Hungary for 40 years, he spoke the language fluently. I was overcome with doubt about whether one can ever learn a foreign language perfectly if one's native tongue is preserved in one's heart and mind with such immaculate purity.

Lajos Kada, Vatican

He grew up in a monolingual family but had started to learn German before his school years. He was not lucky with languages in primary school: He was instructed for four years by a stern, strait-laced teacher who had a propensity to harp on grammar at the expense of vocabulary and pronunciation. He easily understood literary texts written in Gothic script but later in Vienna did not even know that *Stieger*, displayed on lifts, does not mean "lift" [elevator] but is in fact the brand name of the lifts.

When he reached the fourth year of secondary school, the Italian language came into fashion. Following his peers' example, he studied it—besides Latin, of course. At the Pontifical Ecclesi-

---

71.   Currently named Congregation for Divine Worship and the Discipline of the Sacraments.

astical Academy (responsible for training diplomats), he took on English, French, and Spanish.

Among the disciples of the Academy, the ideal of "one world, one language" almost became a reality. The pupils, who arrived from different countries, conversed in Latin. It was only the American students of the Faculty of Canon Law who did not speak this classical language. Prof. Kada had to become immersed in English for their sake.

The Archbishop claims he has always learned languages with a considerable investment of energy. He does not soak up tongues like a sponge. Nonetheless, he is confident in Latin, Greek, Hebrew, French, Italian, English, German, and Spanish.

His vocation as a papal legate has sent him to the most linguistically diverse parts of the world. He has represented his church in Bonn, Pakistan, and, for nine years, in Costa Rica. He has always acquired living languages in living environments.

And what about the level he attained? While he dictated to me in Hungarian his thoughts on language learning, he gave information to a fellow priest on the phone in Spanish. He made appointments in French, reported to his superior in German, and gave instructions to his secretary in Italian. He switched in a matter of moments and with such perfect phrasing and pronunciation that all I could utter in farewell was—in envy and in style—a sigh of "My God!"

André Martinet, Sceaux, France

He is the best-known theoretical philologist of our age. There cannot be any textbooks or monographs that fail to cite him. Whenever I sensed that my interlocutors began to get bored with my questions, I floated a question: "By the way, do you have any message for Professor Martinet?" They instantly became attentive. How would they dare to be impolite with someone who implies an acquaintance with such an authority?

He was born in Savoy, in the first decade of the 20th century, when mass communication devices did not yet help the merging of dialects into a language. Apart from standard French, Savoy's regional variety—the *regiolect*—was still in full bloom. Professor Martinet grew up bilingual. It is no coincidence that he has been heading the World Center of Information on Bilingual Education since 1980.

Hence it is also logical that he chose comparative linguistics for his profession. His doctoral thesis dealt with the sound system of Germanic languages. His teaching career was interrupted by the war, and then by captivity, but he used his years in the Weinsberg prison camp for mapping the pronunciation features of the inhabitants of the individual French regions. Answering my question, he classified his linguistic faculties by level, as follows:

"I speak English at the same level as my native French. When I speak Danish, German, or Provençal, topics of everyday communication cause no trouble to me, but during professional debates sometimes it happens that I have to think of the *form* as well, aside from the *content*.

"I often use Italian and Spanish in my travels; Portuguese, Swedish, Dutch, Norwegian, and Russian belong to the same category—let us call my level a C. I must mention one point, though: I do not make pronunciation mistakes even in languages I know at the B or C levels."

Otto von Habsburg, Munich

If I look down the well of memory, which is laden with experiences of more than three-quarters of a century, the past looks
back from a frightful depth. In 1915, at the end-of-year ceremony
of my first primary school class in Pécs,[72] I received a book as a re-
ward for "reading beautifully." On the book's title page was a portrait of Franz Joseph von Habsburg, Emperor of Austria and King
of Hungary. He was in a white uniform, and he was looking down
at his hands, as if he were examining and weighing everything.[73]

Seventy years have passed. In front of me today is Otto von
Habsburg, the Emperor's godson. When I was a child, I met him,
so to speak, but he does not recognize me. I cannot blame him: I
was hanging out of a fourth-story window of a tenement in Budapest along with a lot of other people in order to catch a glimpse of
the golden-haired boy sitting in the coronation coach.

Otto von Habsburg has brown hair and a thick mustache
and looks much younger than his 75 years. We are talking in a
modest office building of Pan-Europa in Munich. Because our
topic is language learning, and because he wrote in his letter that
"Acquiring foreign languages is a subject that has interested me
all my life," he answers my questions readily—and in impeccable
Hungarian. In the first minutes I have to get used to his aristo-
cratic uvular r's, but he expresses himself with such exactitude and
accuracy that it wrenches my heart to think of modern Hungarian
teenagers' meager vocabulary and fragmentary ways of expression.

A renowned Hungarian historian asked me to try to procure
from von Habsburg some kind of document about his role in

---

72. A city in southern Hungary.
73. Reference to his manifesto "To My Peoples," issued on July 28, 1914.

Hungary's attempt to avoid prolonging the war on October 15, 1944,[74] but von Habsburg declined it. "I do not like memoirs," he said, "although I know that it is a fashionable genre. Indeed, there are memoirs by some who haven't done anything."

Otto von Habsburg speaks German, Hungarian, French, English, Spanish, Portuguese, and Italian. He did not mention Latin, and I forgot to ask him whether the story that circulated in the world press was true. The story was that one of the speakers in the European Parliament started an oration in Latin. Interpreters went on strike, saying that Latin was not among the official languages. The situation was saved by von Habsburg. He stood up and translated perfectly the whole Latin address into German, if I remember correctly.

Incidentally, among all my interviewees in the North and South, East and West, he was the only one who showed interest in my humble person ("Tell me something about yourself").

I believe his good upbringing explains this courtesy.

Ferenc Kemény, Oslo

I came across his name first in the article summarizing the results of the Swedish survey. "The language skills of those asked covered a wide range," the communiqué said. "The upper limit was set by the correspondent who reported a high-level command of 20 languages."

Of course, I immediately asked them about this person, but I did not realize from the name in the English-language reply— Mr. Francis Kemeni—that he was a Hungarian. When we met in

---

74. Regent Miklós Horthy announced his request for an armistice with the Soviet Union, but the Hungarian army ignored it, and he was forced to abdicate.

Norway, it turned out that we were not only compatriots but also old acquaintances.

After the liberation in 1945, both of us were working as high-ranking civil servants. Soon higher authorities found out that neither he, nor I, nor most of our mutual friends, were qualified to manage the construction of a cultural edifice to modern times. When we met 40 years later in Oslo, we spent the first hour discussing which of us had been relegated to a lower position, and when. The decisions had been made, of course, without recognizing whatever merits we had. That's how things were done in those days.

Years later Kemény settled in Oslo with his wife of Norwegian descent, Madam Johanna, who speaks perfect Hungarian; he was a Hungarian language consultant at the university there for a while.

He was born in Buda in 1917. It was a bilingual world; I remember it myself. We used German rather than Hungarian to speak to the countrywomen selling sour cream and eggs at the market, the shop owners in canvas aprons, and the artisans of various trades.

The bilingual environment and the mixture of languages he heard from his grandmother, whose native tongue was German, soon aroused his interest in language learning. He read extensively in secondary school, and he familiarized himself with French and Latin. He did not take classes. He studied Italian on his own, but with English he received help, and from not just anybody. His teacher was Emma Véghelyi, Hugó Ignotus's[75] sister, a highly educated lady of the first decades of the 20th century.

Listening to the radio, he acquired French pronunciation so

---

75. Hugó Veigelsberg, better known by his pen name Ignotus, was a noted Hungarian publicist, art critic, editor, writer, and poet (1869–1949).

well that native French speakers seldom question his birthplace.

(Apologizing to my interviewees as well as to my readers, I would like to touch here on the role that a "good ear" plays in language skills. If the reader is not interested in the theoretical approach to the issue, please feel free to skip these few lines.

My interlocutor mentioned that Mihály Babits,[76] who cultivated the Hungarian language as a virtuoso, had the sense of rhythm only, but no ear for music. Babits much lamented having a tin ear. Interestingly, it has been established by neurophysiologists that the sense of rhythm is located in the left hemisphere, whereas musical abilities are in the right.[77]

It is also an accepted fact [I have quoted it, too] that the ear required for good pronunciation is not identical to the one necessary for music. A number of fine musicians in Hungary speak foreign languages with an eloquent Hungarian accent. I could also mention one of my best-known interpreter colleagues. Her[78] pronunciation is praised by foreigners, and her sense of rhythm is demonstrated by her achievements in dance and in slalom runs, which demand a rhythmic aptitude. At the same time, her musical talent is so poor that, by her own admission, she can recognize the national anthem only when everybody stands up.)

About his own linguistic competence, Ferenc Kemény said, "I divide the languages I know into three groups: those at the lowest level, *from which* I translate; those I know better, *into which* I translate, and those in the highest category, *which* I speak. Adding

---

76. Eminent Hungarian poet, translator, and literary critic (1883–1941).
77. This explanation is somewhat simplified in this form. See the Wikipedia articles "Lateralization of brain function" and "Cognitive neuroscience of music" as well as their references.
78. His or her. Because of the absence of gender in Hungarian, and the lack of an explicit reference by the author, the gender of this person is indeterminate.

up these three levels: I understand 40 languages, I write in 24, and I speak—perhaps not all at the same level—12."

Rating Hungarian as an extra category, languages in the highest group are German, English, Danish, Swedish, Norwegian, Russian, Italian, Spanish, French, Romanian, Serbo-Croatian, and Portuguese. With the latter two languages, his skills flourish after staying with speakers for a few days.

He translates much and in a variety of genres, with a preference for poetry. I gleaned from the periodical *Bábel* (1985, issue 4) that to date he has translated Hungarian poems into 17 languages and conveyed poems from 30 languages into Hungarian. He has translated works from eight languages into Norwegian, and he has translated Norwegian works into 12 languages, with flawless fidelity to form.

I hope the audience will soon have the opportunity to become familiar with the anthology that comprises poems he translated from German, French, Spanish, Romanian, and Russian into English, from French and Italian into German, from English into Spanish, from German into French, and from French into Italian.

In the *Bábel* article cited above, a nice anecdote is recounted. At the age of 20, he showed Mihály Babits the translation of five of Babits' poems into five languages. Our "poet laureate" had qualms about this multilingualism; he suggested that Kemény concentrate on a single language, concentration being a prerequisite for a perfect literary translation. Fortunately, Kemény did not take his advice.

Much later, in connection with a sonnet by Babits that Kemény had translated into Spanish, someone asked him with surprise, "Oh, so you speak Spanish as well?" Another member of the company, Gábor Devecseri[79], replied "Ferenc Kemény speaks *poem,* and this is what matters the most."

He usually polishes his innumerable translations during his morning walks.

This unofficial ambassador of Hungarian culture, who lives in the North, is not popular with Hungarian linguists. His views about linguistic history are so bold and novel that I dare not even outline them. (He rejects Hungarian's Finno-Ugric origins just as he does its derivation from Turkish or Sumerian. He presents this and other singular views in *Das Sprechenlernen der Völker* [Speech Learning of Nations].) But it is remarkable how this savant, who writes in 20 languages, speaks 12, and understands 40, clings to his mother tongue, with anxious attention to the developments of colloquial Hungarian. For instance, he has noted the regrettable decline of the preterite tense, which today is extant only among Hungarians in Transylvania.[80] The way he speaks about issues of literary translation, mistranslation of titles, etc. manifests such experience, such inspiration, and at the same time such scholarly rigor that his ideas should be taught at colleges and universities.

Unfortunately, they are not taught.

Aleksandr Naumenko, Moscow

I admit I am partial to Sasha.

Our acquaintance dates back to 1972. He caught sight of my first book in the window of a bookshop, got his hands on it, became fond of it, and resolved to translate it into Russian. When

---

79.   Poet, writer, and illustrious translator of classical literature (1917–1971).
80.   There is only one past tense that has remained in standard Hungarian (e.g., *láttam,* "I saw" or "I have seen"); the other forms (such as *láték,* its preterite equivalent, as well as *látok vala, láttam volt*) have become obsolete.

he asked for my consent on the phone, I hemmed uncertainly. I thought he was Hungarian by his pronunciation, and I doubted his ability to translate into Russian.

During the years that have passed since, I've often met him and his beautiful Hungarian wife, Ágnes. We always speak Hungarian. Sasha has been confronted with only two obstacles he could not overcome. Once his wife and I tried to explain the "suk-sük" language[81] to him; we failed. The second time occurred at a restaurant in Buda. There was a boisterous group of people reveling with gypsy musicians at the neighboring table. A patron, either a Hungarian or one familiar with certain Eastern European mores, tore a 100-forint bill in two and stuck one half to the sweaty forehead of the first violin and threaded the other half into his bow. Sasha observed the action with philological interest. Then he shrugged. He glossed over it as if it were a typo that had slipped into an otherwise meaningful text.[82]

Out of all those I interviewed, he was the most difficult to engage in conversation. It was only through Ágnes's mediation that I was able to familiarize myself with his past and present.

He was not a model schoolboy; he was willing to learn only what interested him. He liked mathematics very much, but whenever he became bored in class, he pored over Arabic course books under the desk.

When it was time for him to choose a profession, he decided

---

81. A variant of the conjugation of first person plural indicative forms, which is considered substandard and taken as a sign of being uneducated (e.g., *fessük* instead of *festjük* "we paint it" from *fest,* which is based on the analogy of its imperative *fessük* "let's paint it" and standard forms of other stems, such as *keressük* "we look for it" or "let's look for it" from *keres.*)

82. These gestures of rewarding gypsy musicians were ways of showing off wealth, though the tearing of bills was not a common practice.

on majoring in mathematics. He succeeded at the blisteringly difficult entrance examination and actually started his studies, but he
was unlucky—or lucky—enough to encounter Cuban scholarship
students in a Volgograd park. The Cubans, who studied metal-
lurgy, told him about their woes of not knowing Russian well
enough and not understanding the lectures. Sasha turned his back
on his own studies without hesitation and became their gratis interpreter.

In a year he learned Spanish from them so well that he was
admitted as a student of Spanish at Lomonosov University in
Moscow. He selected French as his second language, but love interfered: He met a girl, his future wife, who, as a teacher of Hungarian and Russian, arrived from the Great Hungarian Plain in
Moscow for a non-degree program. Sasha went on their first date
with the determination that, come hell or high water, he would
learn Hungarian perfectly.

He also had a taste of Scandinavian languages at university.
He chanced upon an interesting piece of information in a Swed-
ish-language biography of Marx. The young Marx bet a liter of
Burgundy wine and a sausage with a colleague: He would learn
Persian well enough in 30 days so that he could read it. He won
the wager. Sasha was so intrigued by the story that he, too, took
on the task—and accomplished it successfully.

I was not able to check his level of proficiency in Persian, but
I can relate another fact as an eyewitness. I was invited to Sasha
and Ágnes's home in Moscow for dinner. While Ágnes was busy
in the kitchen, Sasha excused himself: He needed to complete an
urgent Arabic translation. His client would come and pick it up
shortly, and he still had two pages to go. Following the text on
the table with his eyes, he tapped out the Russian translation on

his typewriter as fast as lightning. By the time dinner was ready, it was finished, and he was able to hand it to the courier when he rang the doorbell.

Interestingly, this 100% bookman is more attracted to live speech than dead text. Out of all my interviewees, I think he was the one who harped most on the importance of good pronunciation. ("His facial expression and almost his whole personality changes depending on the language he is speaking at the moment," our mutual friends say.)

He can employ his thespian inclinations even in his native tongue. When he is in high spirits, he speaks Russian in a Georgian or Ukrainian manner to amuse his friends. Does he perhaps owe this ability to an ear for music? No, he is not bad in music, he even likes it, but he cannot reproduce it. Never mind: He has an incredible capacity for recognizing the characteristics of individual languages.

I blushed to realize that he was aware of quite a few peculiarities of the Hungarian language that I had never spotted.

"It was my husband who dissected my own native tongue for me in such a way," says Ágnes, a professor of Hungarian at a prestigious college in Moscow, "that now I can explain whatever is self-evident for me to those to whom this language is not familiar."

It was through Sasha that Soviet audiences became acquainted with representatives of 20th century Hungarian literature. The first book he waded through was Dezső Kosztolányi's[83] novel *Anna Édes*. He related a nice episode about it. Anna, a maidservant, wore a belt made from oilcloth (in Hungarian *viaszkosvászon*). He decided that the division of the unusual consonant cluster *szk*

---

83. Distinguished Hungarian poet and prose writer (1885–1936).

must be between *viasz* (wax) and *kos* (ram).[84] He was somewhat surprised that people in Hungary wear sheepskin belts water-proofed with wax, but oh well.

He translated several short and long works by Móricz,[85] Kassák,[86] and Kosztolányi into Russian. It was a joyful surprise to me that he even translated certain parts of Karinthy's *That's How YOU Write*.[87] Soviet readers appreciated Karinthy's parodies of well-known authors of world literature just as much as the Hungarian public did. Sasha prefers theoretical issues of literary history to translation. He writes poetry as well.

He speaks eight languages (four at the mother-tongue level), and he translates from four more. Otherwise he does not consider himself a polyglot.

Gedeon Dienes, Budapest

If I were to categorize separately those who picked up their languages in a natural environment and those who acquired their knowledge by learning, I would be in trouble with this interviewee. Here is Mr. Dienes's story, in his own words:

> I was a little child when my family was forced into political emigration. I was taken from a German kindergarten and put into a French school. Frankly, I forgot my mother tongue. I learned German and French from my playmates; I picked up their linguistic

---

84.   *Viaszk* is, in fact, an obsolete version of *viasz* (wax), and *-os* is an adjective-forming suffix. *Vászon* means linen.

85.   A major Hungarian novelist (1879–1942).

86.   Noted Hungarian man of letters and painter (1887–1967).

87.   Frigyes Karinthy (1887–1938): renowned Hungarian writer and poet, mostly known for his humorous pieces. An excerpt of his work mentioned above is available in English under the title *This Is the Way You Write*.

errors as well. I made mistakes with such utter self-confidence that, on returning to Hungary, I even corrected my teachers: You shouldn't say je vais (I go), but je vas. That was what I had heard from my playmates.

In Budapest, I got the hang of Hungarian quite soon, but in my first essay, I wrote the word örül (he is glad) as eurule, following the rules of French spelling.

I studied English consciously. From the age of 15, I visited my father in England every summer; other times, we met him in Italy. During a summer I spent in Haute-Savoie, I was so intrigued by the peculiar dialect spoken there that I tried to construct the rules of its grammar.

I learned Spanish entirely from books. I wrote a Spanish grammar for myself, and this job made me so enthusiastic that I wrote the grammar of the languages that I had been using instinctively (Italian and German).

At 17, I felt it was high time for me to be acquainted with a Slavic language. All I found in second-hand bookshops in Budapest was a course book for Slovak. Its declension proved to be so complicated that I changed my mind: Since I was bothering with a Slavic language, why not choose one that more than a hundred million people call their own? I switched to Russian.

After graduating from high school, I had an adventurous idea with a friend. We published an ad in the daily Dagens Nyheter in Stockholm: "Two English-speaking young men wish to undertake language instruction in exchange for room and board." There were many people interested. I selected a family that lived on a farm, where I was supposed to teach Shakespeare's language to a teenage boy and girl. It was not a fortunate choice. The boy turned out to be lazy; the girl fell far short of her compatriot, Greta Garbo. Nevertheless, I came to like the Swedish language so much that— even though I was already admitted to the University of Budapest as a student of Hungarian and French—I applied for permission to stay abroad. I majored in Swedish, French, and Finnish at the University of Stockholm for five months. Hence I can get by in

Finnish. When I am asked something in Norwegian, I understand but reply in Swedish. As for Danish, I can follow it only in writing. I do not know the phonetic rules of that language at all.

When I was an art student in Budapest, I did Turkic studies and Romance languages. Of course I studied the compulsory Finnish, which I became especially fond of, because of the crystal-clear structure of its grammar. I had a taste of Arabic as well, but I got only as far as being able to pronounce the sounds indicated by the script. There were some funny situations that ensued from it later—for instance in Morocco, when I read to local illiterate people what newspapers and posters said. They, who understood the language but could not read it, could not possibly comprehend that someone could read texts without understanding them.

My job as a research fellow at the Cultural Research Institute often requires linguistic proficiency. I represent Hungary at several sessions of UNESCO each year. When I retire, I will fulfill many of my ambitions that remain only dreams beside my current activity. For example, I would like to write the history of free dance in Hungary between the two world wars. I would like to study the semantic boundaries of vowel changes, compile a five-language dictionary of cultural terminology, illuminate the use of the gerund in English for Hungarian speakers, etc.

For further language studies, I picked Japanese. I already know the language in theory. As for those 6000–8000 characters that are required to read old and new literature, I will learn them somehow.

Gedeon Dienes's linguistic autobiography must be supplemented with two more items, even though I know he will dislike my mentioning them.

During the war, he was the driver of Valdemar Langlet, the high commissioner of the Swedish Red Cross. In this capacity, he had the opportunity to help numerous persecuted people.

The other piece of information is of a more personal nature. In 1945, there were very few Russian-speaking people in

Hungary. Soviet people took into their hearts everybody they could converse with in their mother tongue; it was only my friend Gedeon whom they did not seem to favor. Once I could not stop myself from asking them what objection they had to him. I received a straight answer to my straight question. "He speaks our language with a perfection that can be acquired only on the spot. Yet he insists that he has never been on Russian soil. Who knows what kind of special task he had there that he has to deny now?"

I reassured them, laughing, that Gedeon Dienes, who was in his twenties,[88] could have hardly performed any special function in Soviet Russia before the liberation of Hungary from Nazi rule.

Albert Lange Fliflet, Bergen (Norway)

Virtually nobody resides in the centers of Scandinavian cities. Shopping malls and office buildings stand one after the other, and whoever calls on someone should be prepared for a trip that in Hungary is generally made by suburban railway or coach.

It took the express bus half an hour to arrive at Professor Fliflet's home. On the way we passed tall and slender pines. My host was a tall, slender, upright man as well, and not until I received his reply to my inquiry in English did I learn from his response, worded in perfect Hungarian and perfect warmth, that he spoke our language.

This master of phonetics at the University of Bergen grew up in the small Norwegian municipality of Hedestad. Because of illness, he did not attend public school until the upper secondary grades. By that time he had perused the books of his father, a Lutheran priest. Among other books he had browsed was a *Bib-*

---

88.   Born in December 1914, Dienes was 30 at the end of World War II.

lia Hebraica, out of which he deciphered the Hebrew alphabet. This was also how he became acquainted with Latin. When he first *heard* a Latin text, rendered by Berliner Domchor,[89] he was delighted that he understood it perfectly. It was thanks to this sense of achievement that he began reading his father's German songbook.

At the age of 12, he fell fatally in love with a girl. He wrote a passionate poem to her in Norwegian and attached its Latin translation.

He studied Finnish by means of a geologist who lived in Helsinki and a Swedish-Finnish dictionary he bought with his pocket money. He enrolled at the university, majoring in French, German, and Finno-Ugric.

He spent the summer of 1933 diligently studying Hungarian in the alpine pastures of Norway. He then rode his bicycle across Europe to Hungary and took such a liking to its language and people that he returned in 1939. He learned Hungarian at the Debrecen Summer School so well that the course director requested that he deliver a valediction.

To my question concerning the number of languages he knew, his modesty prevented an answer. I found out only through his biography and his list of translations, which includes works from Italian, Swedish, Hungarian, Dutch, Estonian, Latin, and French.

His translations of Vörösmarty[90] and Ady[91] are broadcast by the Norwegian press and radio. However, his greatest service to Hungarian literature was the Norwegian version of *The Tragedy*

---

89. The Cathedral Choir of Berlin.
90. Mihály Vörösmarty: notable Hungarian poet and dramatist (1800–1855).
91. Endre Ady: eminent Hungarian poet (1877–1919).

of Man.[92] The renowned literary critic Per Buvik, who lauded the translation in his review, "We Did Not Know," put the work, up until then virtually unknown in Norway, on a par with works by Dante, Shakespeare, Racine, Goethe, Ibsen, and Dostoyevsky.

How is it possible that the dignified dramatic character of the *Tragedy,* the ardent solemnity of Vörösmarty's "Appeal,"[93] Ady's shockingly novel lyrical poetry, and Gyula Illyés'[94] playfully gleaming prose in *Charon's Ferry* can be conveyed with equal ease by a native of a distant country?

"It is not only a matter of intellect," the master of phonetics replies, "but also of the heart. Because one half of the head—the better half—is the heart."

Otto Back, Vienna

He is the director of administration of the Interpreting School in Vienna. If I were the Minister of Culture in Austria, I would immediately appoint him as a Public Relations Man of all such schools. These people, fashionable in the West, are expected to gain the favor of the outside world for the commissioning institute. Dr. Back is so affable and approachable that he could not only inspire everyone to enroll in the Interpreting School but also to swap their chosen profession for a linguistic career.

He specialized in a rigid-sounding field, graphemics. This discipline analyzes the differences between the pronounced and written forms of words. On the side, he deals with the Romanization rules for Russian names, orthographic matters of the Bulgarian

---

92. A play by Imre Madách (1862); a major work of Hungarian literature.
93. The poem (1836) is considered a second national anthem of Hungary.
94. Eminent Hungarian poet and novelist (1902–1983).

language, Albanian loanwords, and the difficulty of learning artificial languages versus natural languages. He recently summarized the capitalization rules of German nouns in a booklet of 101 (!) pages.

Here is the origin of his interest in languages, in his own words:

> I grew up in a completely monolingual environment. I gained my language skills exclusively by study. My key experience dates back to the age of ten. I came across a Plattdeutsch (Low German) variant of Grimm's fairy tales. I was so thrilled by the similarities and disturbing discrepancies between German and Plattdeutsch that I waded through the whole book. Thereafter it was a piece of cake to learn Dutch.
>
> Then I started to thumb the pages of the book *1000 Words in English*. Officially speaking, I began studying English at age 13 with the fervor and enthusiasm that only a child can have.
>
> The next stages of language learning were controlled by political events. My father was a Jew from Moravia; he did not request naturalization even in Austria…at first out of indifference, but later in the hope that some country would offer refuge to him and his family. For this reason he started to teach me about the Czech language. Although he, my mother, and their compatriots chatted fluently in the vernacular, they had no idea about the structure of the language and the rules of its grammar. I had no choice but to gather from a Toussaint-Langenscheidt course book all the things that I needed to know but that they did not need in the least.
>
> Simultaneously, I started learning French in school, and Spanish at home, on my own.
>
> My interest in Russian was born in a curious way. The Nazi army invaded Vienna. Hitler's propaganda network quickly organized an anti-Bolshevik exhibition, and children at our school were ordered to see it. The Cyrillic letters I saw for the first time made such an impression on me that I immediately had the teacher explain them to me, and I learned the whole alphabet on the spot.

My school career ended in 1942 because of my ancestry: I was placed among the verwiesen, the expelled. I advanced to become a trader's apprentice. Then I learned the craft of a model carpenter.

The new lifestyle involved lots of tribulations but one big advantage—I could spare the energy that I would have invested in studying mathematics, chemistry, and physics in school. As soon as the war was over, all I had to complete was an equivalence course of a couple of months, and I could instantly take the high school graduation exam at a verbilligt (discounted) price. In parallel with the course, I could keep myself busy in an American garage; my mastery of English was enriched there with live, current phrases.

Thanks to my excellent teacher Maurice Kropotov, my knowledge of Russian and French came together so well that I was admitted to the department of Romance and Slavic languages at the university. In four years I received my teacher's degree in Russian and French. My thesis topic was the expression of the concept of beauty in various languages.

If we strictly exclude passive comprehension of technical texts from the scope of "knowledge," I dare not undertake any other languages (aside from my native German) beyond English, French, Spanish, Russian, Czech, Italian, Dutch, and Esperanto.

I must scold my interviewee a bit here: He corresponds with me in Hungarian, and he read all my books in the original. Which other languages he omitted I do not know.

To return to Otto Back:

I am an honorary professor in the Department of Graphemics at the Institute for Linguistics.

I can maintain my level of competence in almost every language I learned. The job I undertook at the Interpreting School makes it not only possible but strictly mandatory. At the school, by the way, I am pleased to report that there is considerable interest in Hungarian.

Some of our students are second- and third-generation Hungarians living here. They often speak the language but do not know the language—that is, its construction and theoretical foundation. Some others are philologists led here by their interest. They are well-versed in the field of linguistics, but they need to be taught the language.

I will supplement Otto Back's autobiography with some personal recollections. I was first invited to the distinguished institute mentioned above exactly a quarter-century ago. I would like to relate two of my impressions of that time.

First, there were a number of blind or visually impaired students among the audience. Their classmates brought them in and seated them at their desks.

"I am glad you are among us," the director said. "While your limited or lost vision debars you from several areas of work, your hearing has become extremely refined. I would hope that there will be some among you for whom interpreting means not only breadwinning but also a genuine vocation for life."

Second, the final examination of third-year students of Hungarian happened to fall at the time of my visit. I asked for permission to hear it.

When I entered the room, a lanky young man—the child of a Hungarian father and mother, born abroad—was tested on Hungarian literature. He was to answer a question: What was the precursor of József Katona's[95] *Bánk bán*[96] in Austrian literature? I did not have the faintest idea, but the student answered promptly: Grillparzer's drama *Ein treuer Diener seines Herrn* [A Faithful Servant of his Lord]. He then went on to list in detail the similar and

---

95.   József Katona: Hungarian playwright and poet (1791–1830).
96.   A historical tragedy by Katona (1819); the story is set in the 13th century.

different features of the two works.

If it were not for the problems of foreign currency, passport, age limit, family, etc. preventing me, I would lose no time in enrolling at the Hungarian department of the Interpreting School in Vienna. There would be plenty for me to learn.

András Sugár, Budapest

I hoped that in András Sugár's *My Open Secrets* I would find the key to how two conflicting traits can fit in one person: the dynamism of a globetrotting reporter and the meticulous exactitude of an arts person. To solve the riddle, I asked him to tell me about the development of his relationship with languages.

> It was Latin that I met first. I learned it with pleasure and ease. Then came German, when I was a toddler. My great grandmother, who was of Zipser origin,[97] taught me German ditties. She lived 94 years and never learned Hungarian properly. Then the war came, and I hated the Nazis so much that I even forgot the German nursery rhymes for the most part. It took me many, many years (and a beautiful German girl) for this inhibition to disappear.
>
> I also responded to Russian emotionally, but in a positive way. We became liberated on January 18, 1945, and the first sentence I learned was Dayte khleba! (Give me bread).
>
> Russian soldiers gave me both bread and love; they even took me to the Russian-language movies that operated somewhere near the Western Railroad Station. I picked up such a flawless pronunciation in this vivid milieu that the officers would gently pat me on the head and say, "Why isn't this little Russian boy dressed in uniform?" Of course, later I had to learn the basics of grammar at

---

97. Currently Spiš, a region in northeastern Slovakia, with a small area in southeastern Poland, where German settlers arrived in the 12ᵗʰ–15ᵗʰ centuries.

the Gorky School.

My knowledge of English, too, had emotional precedents that date back to my early childhood. I listened with my father to the news from the London radio station. The magic eye of the radio blinked hopefully in our cold and dark room.

In 1947 I spent a month in a pioneers' camp at the Yugoslavian seaside. I soon learned how to have a word with my Serbian, Croatian, and Bulgarian chums. In two years I was able to interpret in these languages at the World Festival of Youth and Students in Budapest, and I even nagged the Mongolian delegates until they taught me quite a few phrases of their language. I was serious about learning English, too: I set myself to memorize 10 words a day. My vocabulary increased in 12 months by 3650 terms.

I attended the faculty of law in Sverdlovsk, then later in Leningrad.[98] I struggled there with Indonesian as well as the obligatory English. When I went to Jakarta 20 years later, I was still able to make myself understood.

On returning home I took a job at the translation bureau of the National Council of Trade Unions. On my own I studied French with Ilona Eckhardt.[99] György Kassai,[100] who worked in the same room, taught me how everyday usage defies grammar rules.

In addition to the Italian course paid for by the Council, I took private lessons. I achieved fluency in a couple of months.

At a Leningrad student hostel some roommates (and a pretty girl from Bucharest) aroused my interest in Polish and Romanian. I started to learn Spanish. I also found Latvian intriguing and so had the history of the Communist Party brought to me in Latvian. I waded through it by comparing it with the Russian original.

When our relations with Yugoslavia were renewed after 1954, I industriously read the *Borba*[101] for years. I still read Serbian without

---

98. Sverdlovsk is known today as Yekaterinburg; Leningrad, as Saint Petersburg.
99. A linguist and a translator of French literature into Hungarian.
100. A translator of Hungarian into French; later a professor at the Sorbonne.
101. *Borba* was a newspaper in Serbia.

a dictionary, and I speak it fairly well.

As a television reporter, I need Spanish quite often. I have shot films in about 12 Spanish-speaking countries. Then in 1974 Portuguese became important as well: Portugal, Angola, Mozambique, and Brazil appeared on the stage of politics one after the other. I picked up a smattering of it based on my knowledge of Spanish. Needless to say, "false friends" (words that sound similar but have different meanings) played tricks on me several times. I will relate only one failure of mine. The French word attaqué means "attacked"; the Portuguese atacado, which I made up by analogy with the former, means—at least in certain parts of Brazil—"nutty." Unfortunately, I did not learn about it until I applied the word to a minister in an interview.

The languages I currently classify as active are Russian, Spanish, French, English, German, Polish, Bulgarian, Serbian, Esperanto, and Portuguese. The passive ones include Slovak, Romanian, Ukrainian, Belorussian, and Indonesian. Slovenian is in a category of its own: I never did better with it than reading newspapers.

Why did my exciting and adventurous job not wipe out my need for painstaking accuracy? Maybe the reason is that I never shrank from using books and dictionaries to check the information I gleaned from people. My strict, hairsplitting inclination is coupled with a playful temperament. This latter trait of mine explains why my son respects me as a father but still loves me as a playmate.

Kelvin Golden, London

He is one of the directors of the London branch of Irish Airlines. His desire is to leave this position and find one where all he needs to do is make use of his language skills. To this end, he intends to get diplomas in nine languages within one year. He passed the exam for translating and interpreting Irish Gaelic when I visited. Was it difficult? "The exam itself was not; it just took a long time to find an examiner." In the 77-year history of the Institute of Linguistics, it was the first time that someone had applied for a certificate in this language.

His native tongue is English. He was born in Dublin, and he graduated from the university there with degrees in French, Spanish, and history. In the 20 years that have passed since he graduated, he has studied 17 living languages, one dead language (Latin),[102] and one artificial one (Esperanto). At the beginning of each month, he creates an exact schedule, which hangs above his desk; the schedule divides his time hour by hour. On his shelves are Linguaphone volumes and course books for all the languages he plans to acquire.

His original plans were modest: He planned to restrict himself to Indo-European languages. Bartók's music and his hope for a trip to Budapest changed his plans. He urgently bought two Hungarian course books—the excellent volume by Bánhidi, Jókay, and Szabó, and Whitney's [*Learn Hungarian for English Speakers (Colloquial Hungarian)*, 1964]. Lacking sound recordings, he asked me to dictate the texts onto cassettes.

Whitney's style is fresh, idiomatic, and replete with phrases of the living language. The protagonist is a certain *Szabó úr* (Mr. Taylor), who acquaints English guests with the beauties of Hungary. For example, they visit a restaurant in Buda on their first evening. For the sake of enriching the vocabulary, *Szabó úr* orders a broth, a starter, paprika chicken, a bottle of *Villány* red wine, an ice-cream, and a coffee. At the end of the dinner, he hands the headwaiter a 50-forint note, tip included. The date of publication

---

102. Lomb is referring to Classical Latin, which was a polished written language based on the refined spoken language of the upper classes (roughly 100 BC–100 AD). It did not evolve. Vulgar Latin, a blanket term covering vernacular dialects spoken in Italy, evolved into the early Romance languages.

is not given on the book, but judging from the 50-forint detail, it could not have been written anytime recently.

Mr. Golden speaks fluent English, Spanish, French, Italian, German (his wife is from Munich), Portuguese, Dutch, and two variants of Gaelic—Irish and Scottish. He hopes to reach fluency in Swedish, Norwegian, and Danish within a year. He is satisfied with his progress in Romanian. He spends considerable time studying Polish, Russian, Serbian, Czech, and Esperanto. He has already started learning Icelandic. Bulgarian, Welsh, and Lithuanian are yet to come, although he considers Lithuanian very important for philologists.

He has a kind of practical or working knowledge of Modern Greek; rudiments of Latin are still fresh in his mind. He speaks Esperanto only in theory—he has no one to practice it with.

Upon coming home from London, I found a letter from Mr. Golden in the mail. He asked me to have the Hungarian course books read and taped by a male friend of mine as well. That way he could distinguish more shades of pronunciation.

He also reported two pieces of good news: He obtained a copy of Langenscheidt's *Praktisches Lehrbuch: Ungarisch* [A Practical Textbook of Hungarian] and managed to take time off his job as a director, which he had held for 21 years, so he could devote two years exclusively to language learning.

With such determined ambition (and with so much free time), I do hope he will be able to tackle all the languages he set out to learn.

Julien Green, Paris and U.S.

He was born in France to American parents. They spoke English at home, but when he managed to get to the U.S. at the age of 20 and went to the theater his first day, he did not understand a word of the actors' nasal Yankee speech. He enrolled at the University of Charleston, West Virginia; his peers mocked him by saying, "You speak English just like grandpa and grandma."

Although a U.S. citizen, he is among the 40 immortals of the Académie Française. He is perfectly bilingual; he has translated several of his works from "his father tongue into his mother tongue." He does not believe in the translation of literary works. In his opinion, translation is nothing but looking for more or less adequate linguistic equivalents and—in favorable cases—finding them. He wrote his most recent work, *The Language and Its Shadow*, in two languages simultaneously, and the two versions came out in one volume, side by side.

He has a passion for grammar. His favorites are classical languages. After Latin and Greek, he started learning Hebrew from a rabbi in 1931, and he is still busy with it. He learned English, French, and Italian as a child, German somewhat later. He enjoys the lyrical poetry of German, but he cannot always orient himself in its journalism. His knowledge of Latin and Greek is from his school years; Danish, Hebrew, and Spanish are acquisitions of his adulthood. He disdains Bismarck, who "disdained the knowledge of foreign languages and called it a headwaiter's skill."

Géza Képes, Budapest

This poet and scholar had this to say about his language learning:

> This conversation is the first time I've had to face my knowledge of languages numerically.
> However, I cannot provide any data. It is not possible. Someone like me will understand all languages—at least in writing—that belong to the same language family as one of those already known.

I was the son of a village blacksmith, rather far from the realm of foreign languages. When I heard the son of the magistrate converse with his governess in German, I thought that they were playing some game unfamiliar to me.

I was 10 when, on the insistence of the local Protestant pastor, my further education was decided. I had four weeks to study four years' worth of material in Latin. I passed the exam with a top grade. Even in school I saw Latin as an interesting adventure; I held Latin dialogs with myself. I congratulated my teacher—also my homeroom teacher—on his name day in Latin; he replied in the same language. My classmates listened, petrified.

A Latin poem of mine, written in a Horatian form, was published in the Budapest paper Juventus. I was in the sixth grade of high school.[103] In the same year, I translated Theocritus's idylls from Greek, a language we had started to learn a year before. I also acquired German in school. I had already studied French on my own.

I wanted to become a teacher of Hungarian and German. At Eötvös College,[104] under the tutelage of Professor Zoltán Gombocz,[105] I began learning Finnish and Estonian. I was instilled with a love for the French language and literature by Albert Gyergyai,[106] but I also studied Khanty and Mansi.[107] I collected 10,000 index cards referencing their folk poetry. Of course I studied Russian as well; according to Professor Zsirai,[108] one cannot become

---

103. Primary school lasted then for four years and secondary school for eight years, so in the sixth grade he may have been 15 or 16.

104. Eötvös Collegium was founded by the physicist Loránd Eötvös in 1895, based on the École Normale Superieure in Paris, for high-quality teacher training of the most gifted students, irrespective of their financial means.

105. Linguist, university professor, and member of the Hungarian Academy of Sciences (1877–1935).

106. Literary historian, author, professor, and translator (1893–1981).

107. Khanty and Mansi (Ostyak and Vogul are the obsolete names) are peoples in the Ural Mountains (pop. 40,000), whose languages are the closest linguistic relatives of Hungarian, though both are unintelligible to Hungarians.

108. Miklós Zsirai, linguist and member of the Hungarian Academy of Sciences (1892–1955).

a Hungarian philologist without knowing Russian.

My first Russian translation, of Sergei Yesenin's poem "The Bitch," was included in my collection of poems published under the title Occidental Birds in 1937.

I became a professor at the teacher training college in Sárospatak[109] in 1932, and a year later at the Institute of English Studies. There, among my British and American fellow educators, my "articulatory basis" grew so Anglicized that when I started speaking English, I was often taken for a native English speaker.

In 1943, I traveled to Helsinki across a dark Europe, where thousands of dramas were playing themselves out. I was to deliver a lecture titled "Hungarian Poetry Between the Two Wars" at the Academy of Sciences, in Finnish.

The institute in Sárospatak was later closed by German and Hungarian authorities for being an "English espionage organization"; the professors were sent home, and I was sent packing. I was drafted, but instead of joining the army, I chose to go into hiding. I became involved in the officers' resistance movement. I was caught and handed over to the Germans, but I made my escape somehow.

My first great linguistic experience after the liberation was when the Institute for Cultural Relations sent me to Mongolia. TU-104 airliners did not yet exist; my flight from Budapest to Ulan Bator took three and a half days.

They had arranged the usual protocol programs for me, but when I greeted the deputy minister of culture in Mongolian, suddenly the whole country opened up to me. I felt at home: I found in the language 17 words that are shared with Hungarian.

As the saying goes, you are worth as many people as the number of languages you speak. I have gained knowledge in 25 languages, but all I hope is that I managed to become one person. I worded it best in a poem:

---

109. A historic town and a cultural center in northeast Hungary, famous for its Protestant college.

That's your life—so that's your life.
You lived up to your promises.[110]
In rebellion-induced fever,
in loyalty
and
humility,
you
reached up
to
being human.

Niels Ege, Copenhagen

My Danish interlocutor differs from his fellow polyglots in the way he employs his extensive language proficiency. He translates and interprets to earn his daily bread as well as his daily luxury car and luxury villa. On the other hand, he is similar to the other respondents in that he grew up in a completely monolingual environment and had no conscious relation to languages before the age of ten. He adds that every Danish person is virtually born with three mother tongues. Danes know Norwegian and Swedish almost without learning.

It was in his first year of high school that he first took an English course book in hand, but the language instantly became part of his curriculum and took a fairly high number of hours: They attended six classes a week. This amount gradually decreased, first to five, then to four, and in 1940 English instruction was completely discontinued by the Danish government. Simultaneously the normal course of life suddenly came to an end: Hitler's army invaded Denmark.

---

110. This line is omitted in Lomb's original text but is part of the original poem.

Instead of English, the main foreign language became German, but students remain students everywhere: What is forbidden attracts them more than what is permitted or compulsory. Ege, who had been formerly obligated to learn English, now avidly listened to London radio stations.

During his high school years, his command of languages extended to Latin and French, and after 1945 he was willing to apply himself to German. His involuntary comparison of Danish, English, and German directed his interest toward comparative linguistics. ("Although I had no idea back then that such a discipline existed with this name.")

When he rode to school by bicycle with his classmates in the mornings, they amused themselves by making up English- or German-sounding names for objects they came across—advertising kiosks, traffic lights, trash cans, etc. This race and competition was won by the one whose suggestion had the ring of the highest authenticity. (And I, naïve, believed that this method of "extrapolating" languages was invented by myself 60 years ago in a Transdanubian city!)

His sense of vocation took shape when he chanced upon Arsène Darmesteter's book *The Life of Words as the Symbols of Ideas*. "It was written at the most attractive level of popularization, for educated lay people," he recalls. Ege was highly impressed by Otto Jespersen as well. This best-known philologist of his age is of Danish origin, too.

His father did not like comparative linguistics as a career: He considered it a profession too academic, providing only a meager livelihood. He suggested classical philology instead. Ege thus took Ancient Greek and Sanskrit at university, in addition to Latin. However, classical languages did not arouse his interest as much as a modern one, Russian, did. It was 1945; the first copies of *Pravda* appeared on newsstands in Copenhagen. The student with empty pockets was aware that the paper was very cheap. "The new world that developed after the war was so exciting that I bought every issue."

He was helped through language difficulties by the easy-to-understand style of political texts and a Russian course that started then. Fifty people enrolled. Soviet sailors occasionally showed up on the streets of Copenhagen; Ege joined them, and his knowledge was enriched with current idioms.

In 1958, the U.S. offered a one-year scholarship to students in classical philology. He applied for it and won, and he extended his proficiency in Ancient Greek, Latin, and Sanskrit to Gothic, Armenian, and Old Bulgarian.

On returning to Denmark, he took the exams, one after the other, that were required to receive the degree and jumped at an unexpected offer: Sophia University in Tokyo was looking for a chairperson for the Department of Indo-European Comparative Linguistics. Mr. Ege was surprised that there were 50 Japanese and 50 European students enrolling in the three-year course.

In Tokyo he learned Japanese. Was it easy? "Not for me, but it was for my three daughters born there. Then again, the language is still alive within me, while the children have forgotten it completely, proving that the rule of *easy come, easy go* holds true for every continent and every child." The rule is especially true in the Ege family; after the end of the assignment in Japan, in 1968, they moved to the U.S. for three years.

Since 1971 he has been living in Copenhagen. He translates into six languages and interprets from 15. He feels sorry that he cannot make any use of his knowledge of Gothic, Latin, Armenian, Ancient Greek, or Old Bulgarian.

He has acquired many amusing experiences as a professor. I will mention one of them because it is related to Hungary.

Education is specialized in Copenhagen, and Ege is the one always entrusted with Hungarian students who wish to acquire Danish. He received a pleasant surprise from the first class: The Hungarians were able to pronounce the sounds *ö* and *ü* without difficulty,[111] even though these sounds cause problems for speakers of other tongues. Still, Ege could not possibly prevent my compatriots from using our hard, rolling *r* sound—until the leader of a group sent to Denmark for agricultural training cried out, "Now I know! We should speak as if we were Tasziló counts!"[112]

The method worked so well that all Ege says now to other groups is "Tasziló"—and then it is a breeze.

"It's a Proto-Hungarian name, isn't it?" Ege asked me. It would have been so difficult to explain it that I just nodded yes for the sake of simplicity.[113]

Sascha Felix, Passau

I almost forgot to obtain a West German visa before leaving: I imagined Passau as somewhere in the middle of Austria, maybe because it is always mentioned as the starting point for rowing down the Danube. We do not lend the Danube to anyone except Austria. In fact, our large river behaves there like something rented: slipping between its banks modestly, hardly rocking the boat.

---

111. Cf. *ö* and *ü* in German or *eu* and *u* in French, written *ø* and *y* in Danish.
112. Arisztid and Tasziló are characters in a type of joke about aristocrats, commonly thought to use uvular r's.
113. Tasziló is assumed to be of Italian origin (a diminutive of Tasso), but it is now a Hungarian name.

On the other hand, Passau's inhabitants are very proud of their Danube. Even the receptionist who handed me the hotel room key reminded me not to miss checking out the place where three rivers—the Inn, the Ilz, and the Danube—rendezvous. It was only my shame over my geographical ignorance that kept me from boasting that our little Hungary has a city with a four-river confluence: In Győr, the Rába connects to the Marcal, which meets the Rábca as well as the Moson branch of the Danube.

Professor Felix did not boast about the three-river confluence in his city. He replied to my questions with cool objectivity. I think he was the most indifferent of the interlocutors I had met to that point: a total lack of interest in my humble person. Well, of course my interlocutors were the leading characters, and I just a gray interviewer. If our positions were reversed, *we* with our Budapest temperament would have commented on the rivers and also asked, What kind of a woman can flit between languages with such ease? I hope my huffiness was not apparent when I meticulously committed the professor's statements to paper.

As a child, he said, he had little to do with languages. Yet he was lucky that later he established close ties with countries using the languages he would master. He visited North America at the age of 15 and went to school there. He attended university in Hamburg, Germany. He then majored in Italian and French at the arts faculty in Freiburg. There he had to study Latin and Greek as well, but modern Greek interested him much more than classical languages. As soon as he reached the level of active fluency in this language, he resolved to learn Japanese.

He went to Tokyo purely to satisfy his linguistic interests. He lodged with Japanese families and made contacts with Japanese young people. In general, "One can learn only from living human beings." The next two languages in his schedule, Serbian and Croatian, are very similar to each other; still, he speaks the former well but the latter worse. The reason is that he found friends earlier in south Yugoslavia than in the north. Has he ever tried Hungarian? No. He did start learning Finnish, but he stopped. He found it much more difficult than Chinese, with which he coped quickly, thanks to his knowledge of Japanese.

Consequently, he would undertake to improvise an intelligent and concise short talk only in German, English, Italian, French, Japanese, Spanish, or Chinese.

He is the professor of General and Applied Linguistics at the University of Passau, but he is saddened to find that there is no real interest in his lectures. He has Polish, Vietnamese, Chinese, and Japanese students, but they consider general linguistics an oddity or an exoticism. Linguistics is just like Byzantinology, he adds with a bitter smile.

Jacques Berg, Cadenet, France

I have long known the name of my interlocutor from southern France, but not as a polyglot. First I knew him as a writer and poet. Later I learned from him that he initially planned to become a historian while living in Copenhagen. After obtaining his degree he moved to Paris, where he majored in political science for two years at university. He commuted between Denmark and France for a while; he lectured on particular periods of French history at his alma mater in Copenhagen. In 1968, he decided on the milder climate of France and took a job as a television and radio reporter in Paris. A few years ago, however, he became bored with the hectic city and settled down for good in Cadenet. It was not the proximity of the French Riviera that attracted him, he says, but the perfect independence afforded by a writer's freelance life.

As far as languages are concerned, he knows French and English the best, although he has also spoken Danish since he was six. He is somewhat less confident in German than in his "major tongues." He has mastered Russian as well; he went to the Soviet Union first in 1970. Regarding Italian and Spanish, he says "When I am among Italian or Spanish people, I have no difficulty exchanging views in their languages."

Jacques Berg has written more than 20 books—children's tales, essays, and novels. He nevertheless does not deny his past as a historian and a linguist. He teaches history in Copenhagen twice a year and is currently translating a voluminous French book into Danish. The work deals with his specialty, a 12th-century sect, the Cathars.[114] The drama term *catharsis* originates from the Cathars, he explains.

The history of the Cathars demanded studies of the Occitan culture. Because he is already in the middle of his translation project, he has started learning the Occitan language from a professor. Berg complains that it is not easy, even though it is the 11th language he has studied (including Latin in school).

Juan Alvaro Sanges d'Abadie, London

Mr. d'Abadie was born in London to an Italian father and an English mother. He heard only English until he was five. In his early childhood there was such aversion in England to Mussolini's Italy that his father, a native of Naples, was not willing to utter a word in Italian.

---

114. Author's note: The Cathars were covered in a drama by the Hungarian Gyula Illyés: *Tiszták* [The Pure Ones], 1971.

During the war his parents immigrated to Rio de Janeiro. Juan was five. He went to school there and felt Portuguese was his mother tongue. Then he discovered Italian and Spanish, and he fell in love with languages. He attended a French-language school in Sankt Gallen for a year, and a German one in Rosenberg for another year. After graduation from high school, he found himself attracted most to political science. This discipline is especially popular in France, where they call it "Science Po." He obtained degrees at the universities of Florence and Naples.

In the end, he taught language in London. He was given a professor's job at one of the most prestigious private institutes, where he can make good use of his native-level knowledge of all four languages. During the vacations, he can indulge his greatest passion—travel.

He speaks equally good English, French, Italian, and Spanish. He has forgotten a lot of Portuguese, though it was his first foreign tongue. He has less trouble with Brazilian Portuguese than with European. He has no problem with German in terms of speaking, but he finds writing and reading more difficult, as they require a more thorough knowledge of its complicated grammar.

Mr. d'Abadie attended a Portuguese-language primary school, French and German high schools, and an Italian university. But what native tongue does he profess to have? He claims it is English, alone and exclusively.

Nevertheless he graduated in 1983 with the highest degrees in French, Italian, and Spanish. His achievement is not particularly impressive for "continentals"—as the English call those from other countries of Europe—but for an Englishman this accomplishment is rare.

Angelo Possemiers, Strasbourg

The simultaneous interpreting staff of the European Parliament has 300 members—220 women and 80 men.[115] When I asked who was the most suitable to answer my questions, they unanimously specified a Mr. Possemiers, a man of about 40 years. I could not grumble about their decision, but my heart sank a bit nevertheless. How can we, representatives of "the second sex," boast superiority in languages when we are not chosen to represent our profession? My feminism was also displeased by the fact that there were no women among authors of "interesting answers" on the list of the Swedish *patron* (researcher). (I am just noticing that I actually used the masculine version of *patron* here, even though Dr. Karin Kitzing, the originator of the project, is a charming young woman and a mother.)

When I feel that female equality is compromised, I find myself overcome by a fighting spirit. Fortunately this feeling had subsided by the time I was finally able to sit down with my Strasbourg colleague in a window niche of the lobby.

I wondered how I would get rid of the guide imposed on me as a matter of courtesy by the European Parliament. As a skilled sneak tourist, I am aware that wandering on my own reveals much more of the spirit of places than does the standard text recited with boredom by professional tour guides.

I believed I could get into the European Parliament without difficulty. I trusted my old, proven trick: gliding past all sorts of sentinels with a blasé and indifferent face. As a backup, I had an

---

115. Currently the number is even higher: 350 permanent interpreters are employed, joined by about 400 freelancers during peak periods, according to their website.

international press pass in my pocket, albeit somewhat expired.

I had less hope that my colleagues would agree to a formal interview, so I was ready to improvise. I know that it is not only strangers who grate on interpreters' nerves under such circumstances; sometimes fellow booth partners can annoy each other in the tense atmosphere of impromptu translations, despite having built friendships through decades of cooperation.

As has been true many times in my life, nothing happened the way I had imagined it. At the entrance of the beautiful building, my way was blocked by an elegant man in dark clothes. He told me in a polite but categorical tone that today's discussion would be held in closed session, and even the issued entry permits were not valid. Besides, permit or no permit, visits to the Parliament are authorized only by written request. If I filled out the relevant form right away, he would be willing to forward it immediately, out of exceptional courtesy, to the appropriate party. He assured me that I would receive a positive answer within a week or two.

Where shall one begin explaining to such a polished bureaucrat our passport and currency problems or our itineraries precisely scheduled day after day? I found it much better to keep nodding understandingly, to ask for permission to call my newspaper from the telephone booth in the building and tell them I would be late with my article. He had nothing against that. Thus I marched into the Parliament—and no one asked me how I got to the lobbies, where I strolled around; the cafeteria, where I had lunch; and the gallery, from which I heard the session.

In fact, the gallery was empty, and the debate in the main hall was terribly boring. I thought I would witness the clash of the leading countries on some intriguing political question. No, the topic was how much a member of the European Parliament is protected by immunity. They had to decide a specific case: A Greek delegate had participated in a street protest and was reprimanded.

The English, Danish, Dutch, Greek, French, and Italian translation of the rapidly flowing dispute streamed with such perfect assurance and tranquility from the headphones that I could have stayed there gladly until the morning, listening to it with envy. But I eventually judged it prudent to move on and find the place in the lobby where a lively twittering indicated the presence of my interpreter colleagues.

Angelo Possemiers may have been promptly and happily at my disposal because he was out of deployment at the moment and had grown bored with resting. He translates into French from Dutch, English, German, Italian, and Spanish, but he refuses to be labeled a polyglot.

He was born in Antwerp, went to French schools, and at home spoke French to himself. He was 13 when the knowledge of Flemish[116] became a prerequisite to further education. He knew French in the vernacular but could not read it well. In order to utilize textbooks, he had to learn the grammar. "I couldn't have prepared for the next school year," he said, "had not Latin, mandatory in the last two years, taught me how to parse a sentence."

He will not tell me how many languages he knows. He understands, and in fact speaks, languages of the same linguistic family even if he has not dealt with them systematically. He is sorry that he doesn't speak Russian, because it would aid him in learning Romanian, which has many Old Slavic loanwords.

---

116. A dialect of Dutch, spoken in northern Belgium.

Herbert Pilch, Freiburg

His command of languages acquired in school became active through difficult circumstances: He worked in 1945 as an interpreter at the Malente Naval Hospital. After the war, he obtained his Doctorate in Philology at universities in Manchester and Kiel.

His professor of universal Slavic studies held that those majoring in Russian should acquire one Slavic language each semester. The professor's method was to hold seminars on a medieval Slavic language and its historical grammar: The students were expected to learn the modern version of the language from textbooks and dictionaries.

"This was where I learned how to *study*," he says, "and where I discovered again that the ability to learn languages is born with every infant, suppressed only by the inhibitions of adulthood.

"Apart from my native German, I speak English, French, Russian, Dutch, Welsh (which belongs to the Celtic languages), Swedish, Norwegian, and Basel German. Approximately in the order given here. My knowledge of Latin and Greek is restricted to understanding written texts. If I include languages that I learned but forgot, yet can activate quickly, then I should mention a few more Slavic, Romance, and Celtic languages as well."

Herbert Pilch is a professor at the University of Freiburg. He taught at Monash University (Australia) for a year and in Massachusetts for a year. In 1984, the University of St. Andrews conferred on him the honorary degree of Doctor of Letters.

種田輝豊 (Taneda Terutoyo), Tokyo

I know many people in Hungary who learned languages as a hobby, and when they became older, they decided to draw on their multilingualism to make a living. These people are attracted to professions requiring knowledge of languages for several reasons. First, other careers, such as those in science and technology, are intensely specialized; the young who enter them must tread a narrow path if they want to succeed as an engineer, physician, or economist. But we who are older have an increasing need for broader perspectives, not narrow ones. Furthermore, we are not as quick as when we were young. Fortunately, our needs and skills can match up well with language-oriented careers. Translating, revising, documenting, annotating, and summarizing require being gentle and patient, which age can bring us. We do not have to compete with youth in an area where they have an advantage from the very start: speed. (Yet, interestingly, the branch of applied linguistics that is the most stressful—simultaneous interpreting—is dominated by the middle-aged. Furthermore, these people came under the magic spell of this profession from diverse careers.)

Simultaneous interpreting is a job with high standards: a broad range of knowledge, proficiency in several languages, and years of work as an interpreter.

Nevertheless, when the journalist L. M. reported on simultaneous interpreters at an international conference in the fall of 1985, her subjects included a mechanical engineer, a legal expert, a metallurgical engineer, an agriculture specialist, a research physician, a chemist, and several people who entered this career by the chance of birth or upbringing.

This is why I find it interesting now to introduce someone who has taken the opposite course. Terutoyo Taneda[117] worked for a long time as an interpreter of 20 languages. Then he turned his

---

117. In Japanese, the family name precedes the given name, so his given name is Terutoyo and his surname is Taneda.

back on the profession and established a large conference center with a business partner. The center manages and recruits interpreters, and its typing and translating service delivers the texts of translated speeches and debates within 24 hours. He also edits, translates, revises, and publishes multi-volume congress almanacs.

Mr. Taneda is my only polyglot outside of Europe. Because of his special status, I ask [my readers] for permission to have him speak at greater length.

I met him in 1970, but I had read his book *Fluency in 20 Languages* before then.

As he narrated in that book, his relation to foreign languages started with two disappointments. He was resettled along with his family in 1945, at preschool age, from Hiroshima, which had been leveled by the atomic bomb. The army had surrendered unconditionally, but life went on according to the rules of prescribed Japanese ceremonies. Every preschool day began with the raising of the flag and the singing of the national anthem.

One day, the male preschool teacher made an appeal to the children. "Gentlemen! (sic) If blue-eyed misters ask on the street if you like America, you should say yes, you like it very much."

Terutoyo waited to be able to say this to an American. Of course he would speak in Japanese, since *people* speak this language. However, the occupying army was not interested in the little boy's opinion.

He was disappointed for the second time at ten. He learned in the fourth grade that not all languages consist of symbols:[118] There are also *letters*. It did not surprise him very much; the Japanese

---

118. More specifically, logograms: symbols that represent a word or a morpheme, cf. "4" for "four" or "%" for "percent," as used also in Ancient Egyptian, Chinese, Cherokee, etc. Individual characters are usually meaningful on their own.

language uses a syllabary[119]—in fact, two of them. He understood less well why other languages write their letters "crosswise" (that is, in horizontal lines), rather than under each other as was normal. But he reckoned that these strange letters, too, were only used for transcribing Japanese words. When he completed his studies from A through Z, he tried his expertise on a German story book. Of course he did not understand a word of it. That was when he learned that there are languages other than Japanese.

He pounced on learning them with indefatigable industry and had so much success that he managed to go to New York on an American scholarship for a year in 1955. His polyglot inclinations led him to explore other languages as well. On returning home, he enrolled in the Foreign Language College of Tokyo but left it before long because he found employment at the Italian embassy, which offered a better opportunity for language learning. When he felt he had exhausted all the options provided by the diplomatic environment, he moved to the famous Shinjuku district.

This ward of Tokyo is regarded by many Japanese people today with the same silent abhorrence as the bohemian world of Montmartre was viewed by Parisians in the early 20th century.

I know from my own experience and from James Michener's famous novel *The Drifters* that Montmartre is the destination for the young who loiter in the world with clogs, backpacks, disheveled hair, stubbly beards, and thin wallets. These hippies watch and collect experience of the present. Mr. Taneda soon became the center of this crowd in Shinjuku. Among his casual friends of various nationalities, he absorbed all the sounds, words, and

---

119. A set of symbols that represents syllables.

phrases he heard like a sponge, and then—having recorded them in his mind—reflected them as does a clear mirror.

For those who believe such "linguistic geniuses" soak up languages spontaneously without effort, I include here a passage from his book. He describes how much energy he puts into learning a language, in this case Dutch.

"I got my start in the third year of high school when I learned there was a Dutch missionary, named de Vries, working in our city. Driven by pure curiosity, I looked up the part in the book *The World's Languages* that explained the Dutch language using a fable by Aesop, *De Noordenwind en de Zon* [The North Wind and the Sun]. Then I slung the school's tape recorder—rather heavy back then—over my shoulder and turned up at the missionary's flat. I introduced myself and asked him to read the text on tape. Then I played it over and over, so many times that the sounds and stresses still reverberate in my ears."

Shortly thereafter he read an ad in the "Jobs Offered" section of the *Japan News*: "Dutch family stationed in Tokyo looks for maid." The lady of the apartment must have been surprised when a lanky, broad-shouldered young man applied for the position. After clarifying his purpose, he left the flat with heaps of recordings (poems, short stories, articles)—and with such amicable feelings that he is still in contact with the family.

"To extend my knowledge of Dutch, I turned to the *Teach Yourself* series. It was a poor little book, but it proved useful when combined with my existing command of German."

As any ambitious language learner would, Taneda grieves when Dutch people prefer to converse with him in English rather than in their native tongue. He claims nevertheless that the study of languages is a joyful process in itself, even if its practical use arises only later or not at all. I quote: "I have dealt with a number of languages during the past few years. I cannot glance at my books on my desk without being touched: They have been and remain my faithful instructors. I was interested in all tongues, but I exerted time and energy on the following 20: English, German, Dutch, Swedish, Norwegian, Icelandic, Finnish, Turkish, Persian, Arabic, French, Italian, Spanish, Portuguese, Latin, Cantonese and Mandarin Chinese, Korean, Russian, and Czech."

Mr. Taneda did not reply to my last letter. I sent him a postcard; it was returned with the stamp "Moved."

There is no Tokyo telephone directory available in Budapest. When I find one abroad, I spend hours searching for his address. However, I know that I have as much chance of succeeding as I would finding a certain Mr. Nagy in Hungary, or a particular Mr. Andersen in Denmark. In Copenhagen alone there are 25,892 Andersens in the directory!

Mr. Taneda must have learned Hungarian in the meantime. If he chances upon this book, I urgently ask him to get in touch. I wonder how many languages he can currently speak *pera-pera*— that is, fluently.

Eva Toulouze, Paris

Eva differs from the rest of the polyglots in gender and age: She has just turned 30. She can attribute her enviable proficiency in languages—apart from motivation and diligence—to the circumstances of her birth and upbringing.

Her Italian mother spoke to her only in Italian, her Portuguese father, only in Portuguese. She went to a preschool in Poitiers, France; she attended a French *lycée* in Lisbon; she graduated in Rome. She acquired English in the lycée. She studied German as well with an excellent educator, but when she learned that he was a Nazi at heart, she sent him away after a year.[120]

She acquired Spanish relatively quickly as it was related to the three languages she had already learned.

At 11 she started to learn Russian for mere enjoyment. She obtained her degree at the school of international relations of the Paris Institute of Political Studies.

Still a university student, she became a member, and then the leader, of the Union of Communist Students. She found a job at 21 at a travel agency in Paris; she organized trips to socialist countries. That was how she went to Cuba, the Soviet Union, Hungary, East Germany, Poland, and Czechoslovakia.

In the meantime, in 1982, she enrolled in Hungarian and Finnish courses at the Institute for Foreign Languages. At present she is preparing for her MA exam in both languages. She very much enjoyed the two months she spent in 1983 on scholarship at ELTE University in Budapest, where she became acquainted with several Finno-Ugric languages, especially Mari (Cheremis).

She works for the documentation center of the French Communist Party, for whom she has responsibility for socialist countries, the Far East, and other parts of Asia. Thus she has constant contact with Serbo-Croatian, Polish, and Bulgarian, although her knowledge is limited to reading in these languages.

She is a member of the prestigious French-Hungarian Translation Workshop, led by Jean-Luc Moreau. I am slightly envious. We owe to her not only the translation of short stories by Dezső Kosztolányi and Áron Tamási, but also the French version of *The Wolf's Bride,* the novella by the Finnish writer Aino Kallas. But

---

120. The teacher's gender is not known from the original text.

I will forgive her unfaithfulness: She is translating Erzsébet Gal-góczi's superb novella *The Chapel of St. Christopher* into one of her native tongues, French.

Philip King, Birmingham

He not only comments on his own polyglottism with typical English reserve, but also questions the possibility of multilingualism in general. "Only degrees exist," he says. "For example, Arabic represents for me the lowest rung of the ladder; all I know about it are the various forms of address. My mother tongue naturally stands at the top of the ladder, but if I were to speak about, say, ballet instruction, I would fail even in English."

He had good schooling. He graduated from Oxford with degrees in Russian and Greek and obtained a doctorate in general linguistics from the University of Reading.

What he likes most is teaching English, sometimes in Birmingham, sometimes at a university abroad. Among his main languages, he speaks Greek better and better—he married a Greek. His knowledge of Russian has somewhat faded. "Sometimes I have to suspend being a professor and become a student again," he says. His Spanish is good, but he would not undertake writing business letters. In French, when it comes to everyday texts, rather than academic jargon, he has to look up words now and then. For the time being he speaks Italian, Portuguese, German, and Dutch only at a tourist level. He reads in Welsh and speaks it a little bit.

He envies Hungarians and speakers of other "non-exportable" languages because they must take language learning seriously. He is quite unlike his compatriots, who are made lazy and conceited by their native tongue's being a *lingua franca,* a common language.

At home the Kings speak English and Greek alternately so their children will know both languages with equal skill.

Kató Lomb, Budapest

I would like to place my own portrait in a humble corner of the Gallery of Multilinguals.

A self-interview allows me to mentally retrace the path I have already described. The reason I relate it again is to give guidance to the impatient youth and easily discouraged retirees. My testimony reveals how, after initial failures and stumbling, a passion can be born that imbues a life, ambling toward its eightieth year, with joy and meaning.

When I was a child, it was known among my friends that I spoke the worst German, at the time *the* foreign language in Hungary. Even my high school diploma was disfigured by two bad marks: I did not get an A in mathematics or in German. Unfortunately, the former is still virgin territory for me; about the latter, I have since managed to catch up.

Now, from the distance of several decades, I can see that my initial failures and later successes derived from the same source.

In those days, the life of the urban middle class not only included having a factotum, considered indispensable, but also having a *Fräulein* (governess). My physician father, the pulmonologist of the Workers' Sick Fund, had a predilection toward poor patients and was interested in theoretical medicine. Thus we could never afford the luxury of a *Fräulein*. Yet it was a *must* to speak German: 20% of the population of Pécs (called Fünfkirchen at the time) consisted of ethnic Germans.

That was why I was bound to think up the method that forms

the basis of my language learning even today: starting with the known and trying to deduce the unknown (if *tinta* is *Tinte*,[121] then *hinta* can only be *Hinte*[122]). My peers, who had the correct forms crammed into their heads by their Fräuleins, found my misbegotten derivations absolutely hilarious.

As my parents saw my setbacks, they tried to take me closer to German. Unfortunately, they chose the most uninstructive way: I was supposed to wade through Schiller's historical tragedy *Fiesco*, which was lumbering and antiquated in style even at the time of its creation.

Here I ask for permission to include a paragraph to commemorate my father, Dr. Ármin Szilárd. He began to write the chief work of his life as a medical student, back at the turn of the 20th century, but because of the hard times he had, it took him 35 years to finish it. He titled his work *Dynamische Nervenlehre* [Dynamic Neurology] and published it himself. By the time it appeared, however, theoretical deductions had been replaced by experimental science; thus it did not arouse much public attention. Nevertheless, a few scientists—most notably Sigmund Freud—wrote warm reviews of it.

Forty years later, in the mid-seventies, a noted Japanese professor of physiology, Hideomi Tsuge, visited Hungary. I chaperoned him as an interpreter. When we were just about to see the Institute of Physiology at the University of Pécs, the subject turned to my passion, language learning. Professor Tsuge confessed that he had acquired some command of only a single language aside from his (broken) English. He had studied German for a while, he said,

---

121. *Tinta:* ink (Hungarian); *Tinte:* ink (German).
122. *Hinta* is swing (hanging seat) in Hungarian; its assumed counterpart is meaningless in German.

in order to read the work of a European physician (he did not remember his nationality), Dr. Ármin Szilárd. "I can still quote pages from it," he added, overcome with emotion.

Let me lay this memory of mine, instead of a flower, on the grave of a just person and a just physician.

Going back to my language learning: Perhaps it was precisely my failure in German that made me pounce on learning French with such passion. In French I could start on the same footing with the others. I must have proceeded quickly; I remember I began writing a novel three months later. The work was originally planned to have several volumes, but I completed only one page, and later it got lost. However, I can still remember two things clearly: that I had to look up even such common words as "but" and "only" in the dictionary and that underneath the title (which I have also forgotten) there was a proud sentence I had picked up somewhere: *Tous droits réservés* (all rights reserved).

If I were questioned about the pivotal moment of my life, I would specify the minute when the sweet tune of a Latin sentence first rang in my ears: *Juventus ventus* (youth is folly). Gates to the beauty of the form of languages swung open before me; a way opened to the realm on the paths of which I have been wandering for three quarters of a century with ever-increasing enthusiasm.

It was books, dictionaries, overheard conversations, and later radio stations that teased my appetite and assuaged my hunger when I familiarized myself with tongues in the Slavic, Germanic, and Romance families, and later with Chinese and Japanese.

I have babbled enough about my method of language learning. I would like to add how much I owe, besides interest and tenacity, to coincidences that shaped the circumstances of my life. These accidents always seemed unlucky at first.

When I obtained my doctoral degrees (alas, in chemistry and in physics), the global economic recession of the thirties had just begun. Specialists with several decades' expertise became unemployed. A novice chemist had little if any prospect to find a position. I started to learn English, alone.

As the depression subsided somewhat, I succeeded in finding a job, but I was soon driven out of it—in May of 1938—by the law with the sonorous title "for the more effective protection of the social and economic balance." I used this more recent period of my joblessness to get acquainted—once again on my own and secretly—with the beauty of the Russian language.

After the Russian army's liberation of Budapest from Nazi rule in 1945, my career started off nicely as a civil servant. However, it ended abruptly by the year of the turn.[123] This was good for coming to grips with the Chinese language, but by the time I learned how to move with more or less confidence in it, there was no need for my knowledge: All our relations with Mao's China were terminated.[124] Fortunately I did not know any Japanese, so it gave me something on which to spend my new-found free time.

People often ask me if I am still learning languages. I normally say that for someone like me, learning is not an activity but an attitude. It has become my lifestyle—I hope until my dying day—to select my readings on the basis of which language I become hungry for or which I happen to need. On the street, on buses and trains, ignoring the most elementary rules of discretion, I prick up my ears to all words uttered in a foreign language. In

123. This refers to the year 1948, when the Hungarian Communist Party merged with the Social Democratic Party to become the Hungarian Working People's Party. This merger led to the communist takeover in Hungary.
124. At the end of the fifties, followed by an estrangement in the sixties.

museums, libraries, or at shows abroad, I follow the guide until the exhibits practically return my greeting in every language.

Instead of visiting the theater and cinema when I am in the West (they are usually prohibitively expensive), I read newspapers and hear about the free popular science lectures available. Where I see a multitude of people pouring in somewhere, I follow them. In this way I have picked up idioms at interesting literary, scientific, political, and economic debates. There is no believer who wears out the thresholds of churches as much as I do abroad: Priests of all denominations always speak clearly, slowly, and understandably.

Needless to say, I immediately write down all new phrases from conversations, lectures, and debates—on the pretext of taking notes. I cling with unabated interest to what has always been the most intriguing question for me: *How do they say it?* Unfortunately, what they say is very often different from what our course books teach.

I preserve overheard expressions in my notebooks, which I hide in my pocket or my purse. When in a line—at laundries, shops, or grocery cash registers—I almost automatically reach for them. I may be the only inhabitant of our beautiful capital who has never grumbled about the delay of transport vehicles. If I am lucky, and it takes a long time for the No. 12 bus to come, I may manage to wade through as many as five or six pages.

How many languages do I speak? I have only one mother tongue: Hungarian. I speak Russian, German, English, and French well enough to be able to interpret or translate between any of them extemporaneously. I have to prepare a bit for Spanish, Italian, Japanese, Chinese, and Polish. At such times I leaf through the parts of my diaries written in these languages. I can read Swedish, Norwegian, Romanian, Portuguese, Dutch, Bulgarian, and Czech literature; I can translate their written—political or technical—texts.[125] Once I coped with a ten-line Vietnamese text in Hanoi, in the fleeting time of eight hours. Of course, I do not "know" these languages.

Finnish is still among those to be learned; I have never tried Greek. Learning Latin was and remains one of the great experiences of my life.

I am a happy person because I live for and within my obsession. I have written four books up till now—each dealing with language learning more or less.[126]

I plan to write about one more topic: ways of expressing aspects of action in different languages, especially in Japanese.

It will take a year or two to finish it; the book will interest two or three people in Hungary, and at most another 20 in the whole world. But I am going to write it; I will see to it.

If I live to see it.

Q: When can we say we know a language?

With this first question for the round table, I was hoping there would be perfect agreement among the delegates. I asked, "When can we say we 'know' a language?"

---

125. In an interview with the Hungarian weekly *Hetek* [Weeks] on November 14, 1998, Lomb mentioned some level of comprehension of Danish, Latin, Hebrew (Ivrit), Slovak, and Ukrainian, but she omitted Portuguese, Dutch, Swedish, and Norwegian. In *Polyglot: How I Learn Languages* (p. 49), she describes herself as "being able to speak 10 languages, translate technical documents and enjoy fiction in six more, and read journalism in 11 more or so."
126. *How I Learn Languages* (1970, 1972, 1990, 1995; English trans. 2008); *An Interpreter Around the World* (1979); *With Languages in Mind...* (1983; English trans. 2016); and this book, originally published in 1988.

I added the single quotation marks to *know* because the original question, so simple and unambiguous in Hungarian, was untranslatable in the other languages.

Common expressions—such as *Do you speak English? Parlez-vous français? ¿Habla usted español?*—restrict the concept to *speaking*. The Hungarian term for *know* includes a broader set of skills.[127]

This difficulty was heightened by the definition I presented ready-made to my peers: "We know a language when we can speak spontaneously for five or six minutes on a topic we understand, in a way that our possible mistakes in pronunciation, stress, grammar, or syntax do not hinder the comprehension of our message."

My peers, unfortunately, took issue with my definition.

BACK: The proposed definition is one-dimensional. Let us take my case: If I am to speak about historical, economic, or philological topics, I can do so easily in several languages. But I am not sure that if two Italian workers are arguing next to me that I could make out what they are talking about. Nor could I enumerate the basic parts and accessories of a bicycle—saddle, chain, pump, bell—in all the languages that I "know" according to your definition.

DIENES: Defining a single criterion for language skills is difficult because knowledge not only has levels but types. We can start from the fact that one's command should comprise four areas: (a) reading comprehension, (b) listening comprehension, (c) oral expression, and (d) written expression. Some people are more

---

127. The Hungarian word can refer to any of the four skills (speaking, listening, reading, and writing), but it normally implies all four.

familiar with one; some find another easier to manage. Intellectuals usually find their way sooner in the written realm than in listening.

VON HABSBURG: For me, the criterion of language skills is whether someone can start speaking in a foreign language without preparation. Certainly, it takes courage as well. I could even say audacity in my case, rather than courage. I have hardly spoken any Italian yet, but I already answered in this language to a fellow member of the European Parliament who spoke Italian.

Why does my definition not include literacy? Again, I can merely reply on my own behalf. Reading comprehension has never caused me difficulty, and I can put in writing whatever I have read. Incidentally, this ability is not a family trait with us. My second youngest brother, not Carl Ludwig, but Robert, you know [*I did not know—KL*], finds speech easy and writing difficult.

PILCH: I deem the definition good. It makes it possible to assess the degree of knowledge. However, it fails to consider languages that, say, you understand excellently in reading but cannot use in speech. The level of knowledge is not stable anyway, but rather variable. It rises quickly when you use a language, and then it sinks. How should I appraise, for instance, my once steady, but now much more tenuous, knowledge of Celtic, Romance, or Slavic tongues?

The image needs to be clarified in another aspect as well. Where shall one draw the line between language and dialect? Whoever speaks what is called *Hochdeutsch* (standard [high] German) must still study to learn local dialects, though it will take them less time than other learners. The same applies to variants of a language used in distinct periods. Old High German and Old English are placed in today's philology in the same category as modern German and English, although university students can testify how much effort it takes to learn them.

GREEN: When do we know a language? I think never. There is always something else to be learned. You do not "know" your mother tongue; it lives with you, within you. On the other hand, I know professors and translators who speak flawlessly a kind of *artificial* language. At the same time, I have met people who are led by their natural instincts to the right way of speaking, even if their speech is not flawless in an absolute sense.

TOULOUZE: If I restrict "knowledge" to verbal fluency, I can agree with the proposed definition. However, it is unacceptable in one respect: You must not treat *pronunciation* mistakes the same as *stress* mistakes! If a speaker pronounces sounds incorrectly, words will still be understood. However, a faulty stress will distort the meaning of the sentence. Just think of how, in Hungarian, stressing the ending of a word changes a statement into a question: "*Soha!*" "*Soha?*"[128]

I would recommend other criteria to judge the level of knowledge. You reach the first degree when you can express your message without relying on another language—mostly your native tongue. It is often described as thinking in a given language. However, when you voice your own opinion, you subconsciously but continuously maneuver and make compromises: You say what you *can* say. That is why I can speak of a second degree: when you can accurately translate *others'* ideas as well. Finally, communication will not be complete until you are familiar not only with a

---

128. "Never!" "Never?" In questions longer than two syllables, the pitch of the penultimate syllable is raised and the last one is pronounced in a low pitch. Nevertheless, intonation is the only difference in several cases where English employs syntactic devices: *Elment? Elment.* "Has he left? He has left."

language but also with its underlying culture.

SUGÁR: I do not accept the definition: partly because it is too strict, and partly because it does not take the goal of language learning into account. It can be simply to "get by" on a tourist trip, or to orient yourself in technical literature.

KEMÉNY: No matter how many languages somebody speaks, they will never attain a native level. The one acquired in early childhood has such a special position among language knowledge that nothing else can be placed in the same category. Beyond that, a language learner whose mother tongue is Hungarian has a peculiar advantage to those with other native tongues. Hungarian may not be the most perfect human language theoretically possible, but it is the most perfect one that exists in reality. All other languages fit human thought as well-tailored, badly tailored, custom-made, or ready-to-wear clothes fit the human body, whereas the Hungarian language is like skin.[129]

When you speak your native tongue, you do not have to think of the "how" at all; you can focus all your attention on the "what." The goal of language learning is to acquire maximum *silent* knowledge, which provides the correct form automatically when it comes to active language production.

MARTINET: You can know a language in several ways. Each skill is equally valuable; I could not rank them. Even a little child and an illiterate person "know" their native tongues. It can also occur that someone has impeccable comprehension but cannot speak. For example, I know cases in which children of Breton parents have spoken French all their lives.[130] It is also conceivable

---

129. Naturally, these views are untenable from a linguistic point of view. They reflect only Mr. Kemény's own notion.
130. That is, in spite of the fact that the parents speak to them in Breton.

that someone is entirely familiar with reading and can compose texts in writing, but they dare not start speaking.

NAUMENKO: I think you know a foreign language when you understand not only words addressed to you as a stranger (that is, pronounced more slowly and clearly), but also the sort of speech used between natives, which is much more compact.

TANEDA: The reason I can claim that I know 20 languages is that they live within me even if I have not used them for a fairly long time.

GOLDEN: All definitions fail if you try to base them on one single criterion. It is a commonplace that language competency includes writing, reading, speech, and speech comprehension. If someone possesses a first-rate skill in one of the four areas and an adequate one in the other three, I would accept his achievement as "knowledge." By "adequate" I mean an ability that can be improved to a higher level after short but intensive studies. An example would be when you already understand well the texts that you read, and it takes you three or four weeks of thorough studying and listening to the radio frequently to arrive at the skills you need to comprehend, compose, and speak.

KADA: When do you know a language? Maybe when you begin to dream in it.

FÉLIX: I prefer the official definition: "near-native competence." All definitions below this are too stretchable and difficult to specify.

D'ABADIE: I think you know a language when the shortcomings in your active and passive knowledge do not hinder communication. But there is another condition for language skills: One should know the history, literature, art, and traditions of the given country. In this sense, for instance, the knowledge of

"Belgian French," "Swiss French," or "French French" should be treated separately. To mention but two primitive examples: You should know that *siesta* does not simply mean a rest or a break in Mediterranean countries, but only the sleep that interrupts daily work after lunch. Or, that *Oktoberfest* is expressly the fall festivity celebrating the fermentation of Bavarian beer.

KÉPES: When it concerns myself, I set the standard high. Several times I learned by accident that I was to deliver a speech for some special occasion. Usually I only had time to scribble down some key words. I had success in the United Kingdom, Finland, and even in Azerbaijan with improvised speeches like that. On the other hand, I do not like to interpret. I can succeed only if I can completely identify with the mentality of the other person.

KING: Because people learn languages from a variety of motivations, the criterion of knowledge can be defined only relatively. In this sense, I think the question will be whether someone knows enough to achieve her or his goal.

BERG: You "know" a language when you feel free to use it and are not afraid of making mistakes. You can make use of those little words—*yet, so, well,* etc.—that join sentences.

DEAR READERS: Before calling upon myself to speak, I would like to quote two more opinions. According to Jan F. Finlay, notable philologist from London, you know a language *if you say exactly what you want to say* without translating yourself, and if you understand foreigners who do not adapt their speech for you.

Russell, Mezzofanti's biographer, expresses his view about this issue as well. "1 think a man may be truly said to know a language thoroughly if he can read it fluently and with ease; if he can write it correctly in prose, or still more, in verse; and above all, if he be admitted by intelligent and educated natives to speak it correctly and idiomatically."

LOMB: I accept the criticism. The definition I proposed is indeed one-dimensional. For example, comprehension by reading was entirely lacking. I find reading to be a task too simple, almost elementary, for an intellectual. If one knows a related language, reading is especially easy. Someone with some knowledge of Spanish will understand written Portuguese after minimal practice; someone with some command of German will understand written Swedish. Reading does not involve the ability to speak.

I can cite the example of a Hungarian Academy member who is considered a world-famous expert on two Asian languages. His philological analyses are taught at universities and quoted in textbooks. But when he visited a country whose people speak one of these languages, he blushed to ask a colleague to write a few sentences phonetically, such as "May I have my breakfast delivered to my room?" or "I am lost; please call the Hungarian embassy at this number."

There are two practical aspects I would like to mention for assessing the level of language skills. I would immediately give the certificate of proficiency to one who can (1) decipher handwritten texts, and (2) make sense of pop song lyrics, distorted by rhythm and melody.

There is one more special area: the world of numbers. It is no coincidence that *Zahlenakrobatik,* juggling with numbers, is a subject on its own at the Interpreting School in Vienna.

You can swear and count only in your native tongue, as the saying goes.

Madame Curie (then Maria Skłodowska) went to Paris at

the age of 24. Her knowledge of French was so excellent that she could instantly enroll in Poincaré's mathematics classes. But even after 40 years' residence in France, she returned to her mother tongue whenever she had to multiply or divide.

One of the reasons for the difficulty with numbers may be the general chaos that reigns there. Just think of the order in German, different from almost all other languages: *einundzwanzig* (1 and 20). In England, who knows why, *eleven hundred* is currently beginning to displace the good old *one thousand one hundred.* Perhaps the change is revenge for being forced to use the decimal system for money? Yet it suited their conservatism much better to use the original and official duodecimal (12-based) system. They find their system logical, according to the London-based humorist George Mikes,[131] because 1 pound comprises 20 shillings;[132] 1 stone, 14 pounds; 1 mile, 1,760 yards; and 1 bushel, 8 gallons.

Norwegians ordered in 1951 that numbers should not be expressed anymore with the German (reversed) system but should start using the usual order with the new decade. In the French-speaking areas of Belgium, seventy is *septante,* and ninety is *nonante*, rather than a number thrown together from 4, 20, and 10.[133] However, *two* is the highest number in certain Amazonian tribes. *Five* is, for instance, two sticks broken into two, and the half of another one.

I am ashamed of the one-dimensionality of my definition because I am aware it is possible to know a language in a number of ways. I saw a magician performing on a children's stage in Berlin.

---

131. A Hungarian-born British author (1912–1987).
132. U.K. decimalization took place in 1971.
133. In most parts of France, seventy is *soixante-dix,* and ninety is *quatre-vingt-dix* (4 × 20 + 10).

He distracted the attention of his little spectators from the manipulation of his fingers by jabbering in 10 languages. He conjured
the beautifully pronounced Russian, French, Italian, etc. words
from his mouth just like the never-ending colorful ribbons from
his ears. I came up to him after the performance to congratulate
him, but he did not speak even proper German.

At the same time, the Joseph Conrad phenomenon is well
known. This writer of Polish descent was 37 when his first novel,
written in English, was published, and he almost immediately established a new school of style, according to M. C. Bradbrook.
However, his Polish accent remained till the end of his life, and
it even strengthened with the passage of years. He was at log-
gerheads with particular grammatical forms (such as the use of
shall and *will*) all the time. Aladár Sarbu writes about him in his
biography: "He often spoke Polish while asleep or when he had
intense pain. Around the end of his life, as we know from his wife,
his thoughts were more and more often worded in Polish, and he
even considered the idea of returning to his homeland. Nevertheless, his splendid command of English is at least as impressive in
his best works as his content."

I could cite Arthur Koestler, who left Hungary at eight. He
expressed himself in German, English, and French with equal
confidence, but he was so self-conscious about his Hungarian accent that he was never willing to reserve a table or order a ticket
over the phone.

It may be no coincidence that three of the greatest English
stylists approached the language "from outside." Conrad was Polish, Nabokov was Russian, and Durrell was Irish, born in India.

Q: Which is the most important language skill: grammar, vocabulary, or good pronunciation?

NAUMENKO: I find grammar to be the foundation for languages, what preserves their essence. Whoever wants to use a language should keep its rules fresh in his or her memory. But a native will not understand you, even with the right choice of words and exact grammar, if your pronunciation is distorted. The goal, criterion, and cornerstone of language skills is the ability to communicate.

VON HABSBURG: I consider rich vocabulary decisive. Unless a speaker's pronunciation is distorted to the point of incomprehensibility, possible grammar mistakes will be amply compensated for by the accuracy of terms.

FÉLIX: Though all three factors are important, I would still put pronunciation in the last place. If my car breaks down abroad, those at the nearest garage will understand my problem in spite of my phonetic mistakes. (Then again, you do not even need words for that: A specialist speaks the *car's tongue.*)

BACK: To communicate in a primitive way, an appropriate vocabulary is sufficient.

KEMÉNY: If vocabulary is coupled with serviceable pronunciation, accuracy of grammar is pushed to third place. Uneducated people will commit mistakes even in their native tongues, yet their compatriots will understand them. At worst, they will be smiled at.

To illustrate the above tenet by Professor Kemény, I will include here an amusing document of the usage of functionally illiterate people.[134] The sentences below have been culled by the U.S. Department of Veterans Affairs, a kind of American relief organization, from letters applying for benefits:

1. In accordance to your instruction, I have given birth to twins in the enclosed envelope.

2. I don't get any pay, I has 6 children, can you tell me why this is?

3. Both sides of my parents are poor and I can't expect nothing from them, as my mother has been in bed for one year with the same doctor and won't change.

4. You changed my little boy to a girl. Does that make any difference?

5. Please send me a letter and tell me if my husband has made application for a wife and children.

6. Please find out for certain if my husband is dead, as the man I am living with won't do nothing until he knows for sure.

7. I have no children as my husband was a truck driver and worked day and night when he wasn't sleeping.

FLIFLET: Pronunciation? Vocabulary? Grammar? It is individual sensitivity that plays a major role. As for myself, I am in favor of precise shades of meaning. What won me over to Hungarian and Finnish is that the diversity of their grammatical forms and vocabulary enable a variegated richness of expression.

MARTINET: Every "mistake" is counted as a mistake only if it distorts the meaning of the message. How many times do you get entangled with words even in your native tongue! Your partner

---

134. Author's note: "Unfortunately, the document loses much of its charm in Hungarian: These pearls of style, as is true of puns, are not rendered effectively in translation."

will understand you all the same.

TOULOUZE: The importance of good pronunciation is beyond dispute. In this respect, I owe a lot to the fact that I studied piano for many years. My ears became sensitive to sounds; I learned how to pronounce even sounds that are missing from my native tongue(s).

That may be why a cab driver in Budapest, when he learned I lived in Paris, asked me, "When did you defect?" Or the reason Soviet kids inquired whether I had ever been to the West.

BERG: A prerequisite for good communication skills is a certain acoustic alertness: that is, being able to perceive and reproduce sounds correctly. You will be all the more successful if the expressiveness of words and the musical ring of language give you as much joy as possible.

SUGÁR: Pronunciation, vocabulary, and orienting yourself in grammar are of the same domain. All are important, but the biggest obstacle to communication is deficient vocabulary.

KING: Not an easy question, again! Maybe a rich vocabulary matters the least. Many have dealt with the problem of how many words people actually use. It turns out that even the most educated use only 5–10% of the words in a dictionary. However, if your pronunciation is "perfect," your partner will tend to assume that your vocabulary and grammar are just as good. Therefore, they will interpret as a sign of discourtesy the casual, short forms that you will continue to use due to the limits of your pronunciation. I often suggest to my foreign students that it is not worth seeking native-like pronunciation by limiting your range of expression. It will sometimes warn those talking to you that they should lower their expectations.

DIENES: Although I find vocabulary the most important

in terms of communication, I would commence all studies with grammar. If you can discover (or guide others to discover) the rules of word formation and sentence construction, you are on the winning side. Of course, there is nothing to construct and nothing to pronounce without the words that carry the bulk of the meaning.

TANEDA: I am a perfectionist. I cannot accept faults, whether in the choice of words, or in connecting them, or in pronunciation.

I correspond with a number of foreign friends; I would rather consult my dictionary 10 times than commit to paper something that I am not entirely convinced is correct. Even in conversation, I would rather fall silent than resign myself to something "broken." Imperfect knowledge is the hotbed of ignorance. But I perhaps react the most intensely to pronunciation mistakes. A foreign-sounding accent hurts my ears like a song hummed out of tune.

GOLDEN: The aim of language learning is to be able to communicate. Its precondition is good and clear pronunciation. You can have an ample vocabulary and grammatical accuracy, but if you speak with deformed sounds and erroneous stress, your partner will not understand you.

EGE: To be able to speak, you need to learn how to analyze languages. In my opinion, this means discovering identical or similar elements in what is apparently random. If this skill is coupled with the ability to imitate, then the "Good Language Learner" will not only learn well but also communicate well.

KADA: I had the impression that your partners measure your knowledge by your pronunciation, and they appraise your efforts to learn their language accordingly.

LOMB: They say there are four factors determining the

judgment of people: *appearance, appeal, intellect,* and *character.*[135] At the outset, you react to the first two features: You easily take into your heart someone with good looks and good manners. The other two take more time to assess. In language, experience has shown that pronunciation contributes to *appearance* and *appeal.* Pronunciation is decisive in the first moments of a conversation; it is on pronunciation that you base your judgment of your partner's language skills. It is not until later that you realize that the pleasantly ringing torrent of words possibly conceals a slipshod vocabulary and a haphazard sentence construction.

Q: What method did you use to learn languages?

VON HABSBURG: Not in the classroom, but always through conversation. I studied German, French, and Hungarian as a child, and Spanish and Portuguese as an adolescent. I learned English, luckily, much later, when I got to the United States during the Second World War. Why luckily? Because, to my mind, English should not be studied as the first foreign language. Its initial ease spoils you. And since we are all lazy, we are then reluctant to accept other languages that we have to work hard to acquire. I am very happy that I began with three decidedly difficult languages: German, Hungarian, and French. My knowledge of Hungarian served me well even in Japan. Maybe it was its Asian origins that brought Japanese so close to me.[136] Incidentally, two of my seven children—two daughters—speak good Japanese. No, they cannot make use of their knowledge. They have little children;

---

135. A word play in the original Hungarian: *küllem, kellem, szellem, jellem.*
136. Hungarian, as a member of the Uralic and (more specifically) the Finno-Ugric language family, derives from the vicinity of the Ural Mountains at the border of Europe and Asia.

they are completely taken up with them.

I do not consider reading of decisive importance in language learning. Its only benefit is the expansion of vocabulary. Winston Churchill was generally known to use a wealth of terms even in everyday speech. Once I asked him, "Is it true that you know 45,000 English words?" "It is," he replied, "and I learned the bulk of this vocabulary from the works of a hardly known 19th-century author." I had never heard of the author and later could not remember his name.[137] I learned a lot myself from books by my contemporary Peter Cheyney. He was a very good poet and writer. Unfortunately he died young; he drank himself to death. What impressed me about him was that he not only knew and used English, but also enriched it with new words—most of all, the slang of the underworld of the Isles and of America.

FLIFLET: I always begin with reading. I have never had the opportunity to spend much time in the environment of the language being studied, but I instantly activated all that I had learned passively. For example, I hardly knew Latin and Finnish, but I was quick to compose lyrics—poetry—in them. Success is not a matter of method anyway, but that of emotional approach, affinity, or kindred spirits. To put it more simply: You must love the language and the people who speak it.

MARTINET: I would say that you can acquire more-extensive knowledge—that is, beyond your personal experiences—solely through reading. I would still say so, had mass communication

---

137. According to Richard Langworth at The Churchill Centre, this author may be Alexander William Kinglake (1809–1891), whom Churchill greatly admired. At the same time, he must have gained much of his vocabulary from other works as well, such as the Bible and those by Shakespeare, Macaulay, and others. Churchill's estimation of his vocabulary could not be confirmed by the editorial team.

devices not transformed today's youth and steered them toward auditory stimuli.

Obviously, to achieve fluency much depends on your purpose and pace. The notation of the language also matters. With Japanese, for instance, I can imagine that someone first learns to speak it and only later becomes acquainted with its characters.

The ability to learn languages is inborn in every person. Later it is often suppressed by prejudices, many times toward oneself.

GREEN: I grew up in a bilingual environment: an English home and a French school. This duality raised my interest in languages. I was driven to learn them by pure curiosity. They went into my head easily; I liked studying. Reading? It is essential, even if you live in the environment of the given language. When I am in Paris, I pounce on English-language novels; when in America, I read French, German, and Italian poetry.

TOULOUZE: As can be seen from my biographical data, I did not acquire Italian, Portuguese, and French by deliberate studies, but from my family and school environment. On the other hand, I was led to Finno-Ugric languages by internal motivation. When I started learning these languages, it became apparent that I had the aptitude for recognizing the inner mechanism of languages quickly and precisely. With arduous and assiduous work I developed this talent into knowledge.

I have always striven to prevent my active speaking and writing competence from falling behind my passive skills. To this end, I keep coming up with exercises with new linguistic rules. As soon as I have a little time, I start scribbling. Whatever and whenever. Sometimes I translate long lectures silently, to myself. It is excellent practice and has no risk.

Books are indispensable tools for effective learning. I have accustomed myself to two rates of reading. Sometimes I read slowly and thoroughly in order to enlarge my vocabulary. Other times I read quickly and more superficially, the latter so I can recognize from words the "tricks" of sentence construction. I think it is wrong to start reading only after you are aware of the whole structure of a language! Read to learn the structure of the language. Certainly, selecting the right book takes some discernment. For example, I would not recommend that anyone try to approach the Hungarian language through the short stories of Áron Tamási. However, each act of reading is an intellectual adventure and an exciting challenge to your abilities.

BACK: There is no denying the fact that you can learn a language best by conversing with people. Simple as this truth is, it is difficult to implement in practice. Of course the teacher is supposed to review the language with you—correcting your mistakes—but taking lessons for many years taxes your wallet and does not always fit your schedule. On the other hand, if you expect this favor from friends or acquaintances, it will always weigh on you that you are abusing their patience. More often than not, there is a common language equally known to both of you, and speaking in any other language will become contrived.

A native can correct your mistakes but cannot explain why they are mistakes. Natives do not need to know why: they know their mother tongues instinctively—of course, at their own level of intelligence.

I have a good opinion of phrase books. I am happy to use, for example, a bilingual travel guide whose two tongues I want to learn. These days I happen to be thumbing the pages of a Hungarian–Romanian booklet with keen interest. One language supports the other—and I am doubly entertained.

There was a time in my life when I arrogantly refused all translated books. I would never read a piece of writing in German that originally saw the light of day in Italian or in English! My stance has changed since then. I intuit many features of the foreign language by observing to what extent the translator handled the idioms of my mother tongue. It is exactly these distortions and omissions that give me a characteristic picture of the vocabulary and structure of the source language. Currently I am grappling with Polish by wading through several novels translated from German into Polish. It is an instructive and amusing process.

DIENES: The most expedient learning method for a person depends on his or her age. Before puberty, exposure to a language and a living language environment are much more productive than conscious learning. A mature mind is not, however, content with drills—it seeks rules and laws. It should supplement mechanical imitation and intuition with formal learning.

BERG: I let myself be enticed by the music of languages and the beauty of words. The music of a language is retained and not forgotten by the ear. I think if there were merely two words, say, in German, that remained in my memory, I could flawlessly reproduce the melody of these two words. At the same time, your stock of vocabulary declines steadily, and you must protect yourself against it by reading.

TANEDA: A model learner sets about learning a language by studying a beginners' course book and a dictionary. He learns 300 model sentences by heart, approximately 1500 words. He writes them in a little notebook, which he always keeps in his pocket. To become fluent, he holds lengthy dialogues with himself. Even for the languages he knows well, if he needs them for a meeting the next day, he will talk to himself.

He goes to the movies with a tape recorder; he does not even glance at the subtitles on the screen. At home, he records texts of radio performances. He plays these tapes innumerable times. He looks for pen pals by way of newspaper advertisements. He considers the replies a rich storehouse of living idioms, and he learns long sentences by heart.

He is a great adherent of *scribbling*. When reading, talking, or making phone calls, he invariably has a slip of paper in front of him and a pencil in his hand. He jots down words, constructs sentences, and doodles pictures. "If humankind chose drawing at the dawn of culture," he says, "why not leave a written trace of speaking, a higher degree of self-expression?" Sometimes—strictly for his own use—he commits entire poems to paper: a Norwegian sonnet about an imaginary snowy landscape or a Spanish poetic fantasy without rhymes. He carefully preserves these documents; now and then he takes them out again. That is what lets him monitor how much he has progressed in the language being studied.

GOLDEN: I begin by skimming through a grammar book briefly; thus I gain an overall view of the morphology and syntax of the language. It is nothing but a skeleton, to be covered with flesh by reading as well as listening to the radio and records. I start by reading magazines, then dailies, and I never stop doing so. Books are essential tools for learning, and they are sometimes the only devices for maintaining one's knowledge.

EGE: There is something unnatural in every language-learning process. Children learn their mother tongues like toddling on two legs. If you start learning a foreign language as an adult, you must acquire it *walking backward,* and what is more, not on a smooth terrain but on a rather rough one. There are psychological and biological obstacles—prejudices and inhibitions—blocking the way to proceed.

You must overcome lots of ingrained habits that have become your second nature; you must force yourself to take up new—I would almost say unnatural—routines.

At first I believed that I needed native teachers to solve the difficulties. Then I realized it was not the best method. Native German or English speakers have never studied their mother tongues; they do not feel the pitfalls and cannot explain them. A virtuoso pianist to whom music is an innate, natural medium is not a good instructor of music. A Paderewski[138] is not good at teaching beginners. Danish is my mother tongue, yet I have truly "known" it only since I had to find answers to the questions of my Japanese students.

LOMB: As we are already in Scandinavia, let me come up with a snowy experience of mine that rhymes with this statement. True enough, it did not happen in Scandinavia but in a little village in Austria. I was a novice skiier on a skiing trip. Somehow I found myself on the peak of a frighteningly steep mountain. For a while I stood blinking, scared, stamping my feet, and staring at the valley that seemed inaccessibly distant. A typical alpine young man stopped near me.

"How will I get down there?" I asked, with chattering teeth.

"Well, why don't you just ski down?" the youth said, staring at me in amazement. He must have learned walking and skiing at the same time.

NAUMENKO: What I found to be an immense help was the radio. Sometimes I tape-record performances, and I listen to them many times. Reading? I begin in the very first minute, and

---

138. Ignacy Jan Paderewski (1860–1941), acclaimed Polish pianist, composer, diplomat, and politician.

I never stop.

KADA: I consider dialogues between people (questions and answers) the fastest and most expedient way.

D'ABADIE: In my opinion, you should first acquire a solid grammar foundation in school. Then arrange the language environment around you, possibly abroad. I heartily recommend learning half an hour before sleep. Sleeping is a subconscious state that draws from the experience directly preceding the dream. Recently acquired information becomes firmly rooted and consolidated.

KEMÉNY: Reading is the major and most valuable source of language acquisition. There are more fashionable methods—among them the "direct" method, built on correct forms aurally perceived and practiced by rote. Fairly modest needs can be satisfied with the direct method, but I would caution the ambitious against this one-sided sort of learning.

I find the theoretical instruction of the grammar of one's mother tongue unnecessary at a primary school level, but I deem linguistic rules illustrated with practical and well-chosen examples desirable indeed.

FÉLIX: I strove to acquire my tongues in the target country—what is more, by residing with families rather than in hotels.

As far as books are concerned, I am bound to read constantly in all my languages. That is the only way I can orient myself in the technical literature. However, I do not consider reading ideal from the point of view of language learning. Book characters often speak an artificial language that is different from what we use in everyday life. In fact, I find crime stories the most suitable. Curiosity prevents one's attention from flagging, and the author endeavors to make the characters speak in a manner typical of

172 / HARMONY OF BABEL

their kind and therefore in diverse ways.

KING: Learners should first be acquainted with the structure of the language: the basics of grammar. Then they should procure some newspaper, book, or LP that interests them.

I can memorize words only if I see them written; this rule also applies to words in languages, such as Persian, whose writing systems cause much anguish. As a professor, I encounter many foreign students, and I have many opportunities to speak with them, but I see a great advantage to books in that reading enables *me* to control the rate, in contrast to a conversation, where the rhythm is dictated by the *partner*. In addition, I can pocket a book and take it to bed, which I can hardly do with a human being.

KÉPES: I familiarize myself with a new language by selecting a novel and launching into reading it. By the time I get to the end of the volume, I know nearly everything to be known about the given language. I read conscientiously; I look up every unknown word in the dictionary. I take self-testing seriously anyway. If I become unsure, for example, of the stress of a word, I am not loath to investigate it until my doubt is dispelled.

LOMB: The most expedient way, of course, is being born in the target country. Or, if you have already missed this opportunity, to complete at least part of your primary and/or secondary school there. Such schooling is a mere dream for most learners, however. What remains, then, is formal learning (taking classes) with proven, intellectually vigorous supplements, primarily those that are the most accessible: books.

I cannot resist the temptation: I must relate an episode I participated in 33 years ago. That was when the People's Republic of China resolved to offer adult education.

To acquaint themselves with proven methods and choose the

best of them, they sent a three-person delegation to socialist countries in Europe. I was the one to chaperone the group in Hungary.

The Hungarian organizer of the study tour, the Institute for Cultural Relations, compiled for them programs of a hundred and 20 minutes. From 8:00 AM to 10:00 AM, the Chinese heard a folk choir; from 10:00 AM to noon, a hobbyists' theatrical rehearsal; from noon to 2:00 PM, an amateur dance group.

We were to present ourselves to [the writer and politician] Péter Veres so that our guests could learn how to teach the art of writing to the gifted youths of the population, which back then [1955] was only several million [Lomb's original figure for the gifted youths—800 million—is not accurate]. We explained the problem, and he replied with a single word: "Read!"

I pointed to my watch in despair: Out of the 120 minutes allotted to the sharing of his expertise, only one had passed. Uncle Péter grasped wherein the trouble lay. He gave a twist to his mustache and added: "Read *a lot!*"

I could not provide any better advice to language learners.

Q: Has it ever happened to you that you started learning a language but could not cope with it?

GOLDEN: No, it has not.

DIENES: I could not learn Arabic words. In Arabic, vocabulary is built on consonants, and grammar is built mainly on vowels. I did not get further than reading. I did not try Hebrew, but I think the situation would be the same with it, too.

EGE: Ten years ago I set about studying the Basque language and two years later, Thai. I did not succeed in learning either. Both are more difficult than average, and my motivation did not

174 / HARMONY OF BABEL

rise to the occasion. I failed with Thai because I could not handle its curious alphabet.

FÉLIX: I attempted Finnish, but I could not manage it. I actually gave it up.

KADA: I have always intended to acquire one or two Slavic languages. Because of lack of time, I did not succeed.

POSSEMIERS: I picked up much of my Spanish during my childhood vacations, but later I thought I had forgotten it for good. Later, as an adult, I took it up again, and I was surprised to find that all I had once known came back to me—but at a much higher level.

On the other hand, I failed with Russian. It was the first time I had encountered a language that adds prefixes and suffixes. It was beyond me; I gave it up after a while.

SUGÁR: When I do not use a language for a long time, it fades, as did Indonesian, or leaves me, as did Latin. I do not speak Arabic, either: Why should I learn it when Alajos Chrudinák[139] has mastered it?

BACK: Whenever I failed, it was always because of lack of diligence or lack of motivation.

TANEDA: I was motivated to learn Persian by a dramatic event. As a sophomore, I caught sight of an Iranian girl at a Roppongi[140] teahouse. I immediately dashed off to buy Lambton's *Persian Grammar*. I skimmed through it in record time—five months. Even later, I strove to practice the language with scholarship students in Tokyo. I kept reading the daily papers and journals sent by the Iranian embassy, as well as the Persian volume of the *Teach Yourself* series. Unfortunately, before any of my endeav-

---

139. Hungarian journalist and television personality (1937–).
140. A district of Tokyo.

ors could come to fruition, I became so engaged with other duties that Persian sank into obscurity. Sometimes I take the trouble to try to revive my—constant but loose—relation with it by means of the Beijing Radio broadcast to Iran.

TOULOUZE: Acoustic alertness—that is, the ability to distinguish and imitate new sounds—totally failed me when I tried to reproduce Chinese and Arabic sounds. In fact, I soon gave up experimenting.

LOMB: With certain languages, the effort invested in studying them was out of proportion with the results I reaped. It usually came down to two reasons: Either no known language gave me a clue to the new one (as in the case of Finnish), or the new tongue resembled one already spoken to such a degree that all my effort was taken up with separating them (as with Spanish and Portuguese).

Q: What connection do you see between age and language learning? Is your knowledge decreasing with age?

BACK: I find it more difficult to remember new words now than in my youth. I am a great admirer of poetry: over time I have stored countless poems in my mind. I can still recite most of them even today. Recently, I resolved to complement my repertoire with a Hölderlin poem. I actually learned it, but the next day I did not remember a word of it. Another example: It occurred to me that I would learn the names of Persian months. I studied them for days; I forgot them in hours.

But an older brain also has advantages in terms of language learning: It has something to draw from, and it can manage better whatever it knows.

I was good at Latin as a student; words went into my head especially fast. However, I had trouble with texts. Then decades passed, I picked up the same texts again, and to my utter amazement, I had no problem translating them. I was aided by the practice I had gained in the meantime.

If a language fades in my mind over time, I read *Frauenromans*, novels for and about women, to refresh it. (They are also known as *colportage* novels as they are sold at newsagents and on street corners.) I do not consider crime stories suitable for this purpose; their language is generally too difficult.

KEMÉNY: As long as I am alive and kicking, I plan to extend my command of languages. My program includes Hebrew, Arabic, Chinese, and Finnish so that I can draw from linguistic resources as broad as possible.

VON HABSBURG: I do not think age plays a very important role in language learning. The frequency of exposure is of much higher importance. I, unfortunately, seldom use Hungarian. A fellow member of the European Parliament is a French citizen of Hungarian descent from Transylvania.[141] I seize every opportunity to listen to his luscious and savory Hungarian speech.

KING: Age and language learning? Well...I do not really know. I started learning Spanish at 36; I had no problem with it. Nor did I have problems with Greek, which I began at 20. Five years later I embarked on Arabic, which proved considerably more difficult.

EGE: When I do not deal with a language for a while, I usu-

---

141. Gustave Pordea (1916–2002), originally a citizen of Romania. Pordea was a member of the European Parliament from 1984 to 1989 (Haas, 1992).

ally get down to brass tacks.[142] This is what I consider the best method to refresh faded knowledge: I approach the language as if I am encountering it for the first time. It hardly ever takes me more than two or three days to get to my previous level.

FLIFLET: Luckily, my pronunciation does not wear off with time, and I do not acquire a new language with more difficulty than in my youth. I need less time to make a general picture of a new tongue: My ability to overview has definitely improved. On the other hand, I find it more difficult to memorize new words, even though my targeted memory has always been a source of pride for me. Sometimes I entertain my friends by asking one of them to tell me the day, month, and year he or she was born, and I tell them which day of the week the date was. Interestingly, the trick usually works only if the person was born in a summer month. Why—I do not know.

BERG: My command of languages has not decreased, but my language-learning skills have deteriorated. Just like any other skill.

GOLDEN: The more mature my mind becomes, the easier learning is for me. I cannot even imagine it otherwise.

FÉLIX: My language-learning skills increase in parallel with my years. You learn how to learn while studying languages. You develop a routine: It is easier to increase your existing knowledge by adding new pieces.

The more experience you have with languages, the easier it is to eliminate the mistakes you must have made with your first: thinking in your mother tongue and involuntarily translating the foreign language word for word. Unfortunately, even language

---

142. This phrase is given by the author in English, perhaps for the perceived lack of a suitable Hungarian equivalent.

education in schools steers students in this direction.

DIENES: Age has a crucial impact on the effectiveness of learning. From age zero to six, a child has no idea of learning a language (or even two or three): He or she accepts and instinctively imitates everything. The subsequent six or eight years is the age of protesting: An adolescent is indifferent or even rebellious toward any new languages. To put it in the terms of dialectic: The *thesis* period of childhood and the *antithesis* of adolescence are followed by the *synthesis* in late teenage years—acknowledging the importance of language skills. We hope the late teens also bring along the assiduity required.

On how learning ability develops in later years, I do not have experience. But I am looking forward to my retirement: I want to learn Japanese.

GREEN: I have always learned easily. I have always liked to learn. The more I have lived, the simpler I find studying.

D'ABADIE: As you grow older, your retentive memory keeps shrinking, and your tongue keeps thickening. If you do not use a language, your knowledge of it slowly starts to decline, even your native tongue. However, one normally swears—and allegedly dreams—in the language acquired in childhood.

TOULOUZE: My peers and I can hardly express our views on this matter yet. All I can say about myself is that I acquired languages as a child in an *impressionistic* manner, but from my teenage years on I studied consciously and regularly. A child has no awareness of national identity, and to be accepted by a community of playmates, he or she will instinctively imitate them. As the tendency to assimilate and imitate decreases, conceptual ability improves, which is an important element of language learning, among other things.

KÉPES: Neither my knowledge, nor my learning skills, have lessened during the decades. I still have considerable learning plans ahead. For instance, I would like to begin modern Turkish. I have been translating from Old Turkish since 1954; now I will add the modern version of the language. I will also learn to speak it. Why? Because I want to stay young.

MARTINET: I acquired active knowledge of each of my languages before 30. But I am convinced that one can learn *understanding* and *writing* at any age—right until senility sets in.

LOMB: Languages currently needed are always in the front, and those unused are relegated to the background. If I have to employ one of them, I refer to my entries in that language in my diary. The experience I have lived through, evoked by my entries, and the renewed emotional-affective background, rapidly refresh my faded knowledge.

Of course, I have to pull myself together at the very beginning of a conversation or an interpreting session, but *using* the language catalyzes recollection.

Activating the pieces of knowledge forgotten over time is somewhat like cleaning the house. Things considered lost turn out to have simply rolled off somewhere: under a bookcase or into floor gaps. You dig the item out, clean it, are happy about it, and then you lose track of it again—until the next cleaning.

When does the brain become too old to accept a new language? I beg your pardon: How should I know? I am not even 80 yet!

Q: Does Latin have a present? Will Esperanto have a future?

KEMÉNY: Latin is a precious treasure of the past, but it does not have a good structure. It is rigid; it does not provide an opportunity to coin new words. It was a straitjacket in Hungarian schools for a thousand years. It is tragic that when Latin stepped off the stage of European culture as a *lingua franca*, it was not Italian that took its place but French. Italian is very close to Latin and, thanks to its lucid articulation and crystal clear sounds, it could have soon become the standard in every country. It began to play an important role in diplomacy and commerce back in the 16th century, but it was driven back by Bourbon imperialism, which forced its own language on Europe.

I would deem it desirable to have a well-constructed, artificial, international auxiliary language. It is quite a shame that the proposed reforms were rejected at the Esperanto Congress in 1894, 157 votes to 107, maintaining the completely unnecessary agreement between adjectives and nouns. For this reason, "a good boy" is *bona knabo*, the same in the accusative (him) is *bonan knabon*, "good boys" is *bonaj knaboj*, and its accusative plural (them) is *bonajn knabojn*.

It is characteristic of human folly that even though Zamenhof himself, the father of Esperanto, voted for the changes, it was not the reformed Esperanto that became victorious but the old one.[143]

As a punch line, let me cite the response given by Churchill when he was asked whether one should endeavor to eliminate multilingualism, and whether all peoples should speak the same language. "Of course," the old politician said, "English!"[144]

VON HABSBURG: I am very fond of Latin. Not just for

---

143. Z. later rejected the whole project and referred to 1894 as a wasted year.
144. This must be one of the numerous bogus quotations attributed to Churchill. Though W.C. did champion the use of "basic English," he never wished to eliminate other languages. Quite the opposite: In 1906, supporting the establishment of Taal as the language for Boer inhabitants of South Africa, he said, "The recognition of their language is precious to a small people."

the language itself, but also for the crystal-clear logic of its grammar: It teaches one how to think. I know little about Esperanto; it does not particularly attract me. I would definitely deplore its being taught in school as the first foreign language. Its excessive simplicity accustoms one to comfort, and an average child is even lazier than an average adult.

MARTINET: As long as most academic accomplishments are born in English-speaking countries, it will be difficult to elevate another tongue to the rank of a common language. And it seems English dominance will last for some time.

Latin? What people should be taught is how to coin new international phrases *correctly,* based on Latin (and Greek). For example, I am annoyed to find "the ability to speak several languages" expressed as *multilingualism,* whereas the proper form is *plurilingualism.*[145]

Esperanto, after a few initial mistakes, succeeded in proving its viability, but its spread is hampered by inertia in league with malevolence. I am in favor of Esperanto, yet I do not attempt to acquire it. I do not believe that it has much of a chance of becoming adopted by any number of people.

PILCH: I consider Latin important for anyone studying any branch of European culture at a university or college. For others—such as an Islamic theologian, a Korean pilot, or a German tour guide—I see no point in it.

I have no experience with Esperanto. I do not think it would

---

145. Author's note: I offer a polite rectification because I used the incorrect form in a letter to Mr. Martinet. [Translator's note: To distinguish the two terms, one can say that *multilingualism* applies to a society and *plurilingualism* to an individual. *Multus* means "many" in Latin, whereas *plus* (genitive: *pluris*) is its comparative, "more." There is little reason to denounce either in terms of grammar. There are many compounds coined with the Latin prefix *multi-*.]

be competitive now or in the future with the current *lingua franca,* English, or with Russian.

English was made a common language by the prestige of the U.S. If this prestige rises, the significance of the language will rise; it if wanes, the spread of the language will wane.

GREEN: Esperanto is an inspiring idea to me. Unfortunately, just like other artificial languages, it simply lacks *life.*

Each national language is a reflection of the achievements and suffering of bygone generations. A common tongue might contribute to the reduction of the danger of war, but, in my perception, it belongs to the realm of utopias.

KING: The knowledge of Latin is dispensable, but it has an intellectual *value.* It [here King changes from English to French] not only advances the study of all Romance languages, but also advances the comprehension and memorization of English terms.

What about Esperanto? It is an interesting hobby but unfortunately nothing more.

SUGÁR: I am a heretic with respect to Latin: I do not see its necessity. On the other hand, I believe in Esperanto. Its grammar is simple, it sounds beautiful, and it provides unlimited opportunity for linguistic derivation.[146]

Sometimes I hear it is a hybrid language—but are there any pure languages? An average person—a postman or a train conductor—can acquire it in a few months. Horthy[147] and his associates, recognizing that the language was popular among the working class, placed informants within the Esperanto movement to col-

---

146. For example, *sana:* healthy, *sano:* health, *sanas:* am/are/is healthy, *sanigi:* to cure, *saniĝi:* to recover, *sanilo:* medicine, *malsana:* sick, *malsano:* disease, *malsaniĝi:* to fall ill, *malsanulejo:* hospital, etc. All come from the same root.
147. Miklós Horthy: regent of the Kingdom of Hungary, 1920–1944.

lect information on workers.

It is a commonplace how much it would accelerate and facilitate political negotiations. Were its spread not hindered by national egoism and self-interest, government expenses could be reduced by one billion dollars a year. Esperanto would eliminate the unjustified advantage held by someone who gets to speak his or her native tongue with those who speak it as a foreign language.

NAUMENKO: I consider Latin important: It is a precondition for understanding the classical world. I have no experience whatsoever with Esperanto.

TOULOUZE: Is Latin necessary? What can I answer as a child of Italian and Portuguese parents, raised in France? If students come across this language with its complex structure at the age of 10 or 11, they will learn the others more easily.

But I must admit that Russian, with its similarly colorful and complex grammar, is equally suitable for this role. The fact that parents and children in Hungary do not recognize the value of Russian is not a fault of the Russian language.[148] From age 16 onward, the importance of Latin lies more in broadening one's cultural horizon.

Esperanto? When it comes to an intermediary language, English springs to one's mind first. But which English? As a participant in international conferences, I dare say that the English employed by delegates has little to do with Shakespeare's language or even the English used by Britons.

Although Esperanto does not attract me personally, I have utmost respect for its adherents who fight to produce a common denominator of communication. The political significance of this

---

148. Learning Russian was mandatory in Hungary until 1989 and thus was not generally popular.

humanistic endeavor is shown eloquently by the last three world congresses, held in Budapest, Vancouver, and Beijing.[149]

FÉLIX: I am a sworn enemy of teaching Latin. It is absolutely extraneous for the average person. Even among philologists, it is needed only by diachronic (historical) linguists, who examine the change of one language through consecutive periods.

Latin played a very important role for a long time in German high schools; they wished to bring up youth to assume a "Roman character" by having them read Latin authors. The plan, of course, did not succeed back then, but it would be downright ridiculous today.

In the decades of the Warsaw Pact[150] and the North Atlantic Treaty,[151] one cannot control the fate of nations by Julius Caesar's principles. Instead, English, Russian, Spanish, and Chinese should be encouraged.

As far as Esperanto is concerned: Of course, I would find its spread beneficial from a political point of view. In the European Parliament, which currently grapples with 10 languages,[152] there was even a plan to introduce Esperanto as a working language. The plan immediately failed due to national selfishness.

If I view the question as a linguist: I like its simple morphology, the elimination of conjugation, and the abolition of grammatical genders. Proponents advocate it as being easy to acquire. These claims are undoubtedly true for people familiar with Romance languages: French, Italian, Spanish, etc. At the same time,

---

149. The World Congress of Esperanto has been held since 1905. From 1983 to 1986, it was convened in Budapest, Vancouver, Augsburg, and Beijing.
150. Established in 1955 between communist states in Eastern Europe.
151. Signed in 1949, the treaty founded NATO.
152. Ten languages from 1986 to 1995. As of March 2018, there are 24 official languages. English, French, and German are the procedural languages.

I do not know whether, for example, a Japanese could cope with it easier than with English.

KADA: Is Latin necessary? The entire history of Europe is *Latinate!* For example, Latin was spoken in the Parliament of Hungary until the middle of the 19th century. When the Church permitted the use of national languages, they opined that Latin would remain the language of the liturgy. Today, unfortunately, even young priests do not have a good command of it. It is a pity because this classical tongue is excellent for teaching logical thinking. It also provides a foundation for learning many national languages. Of course Latin, just like any other language with a long history, is quite replete with forms and variants. For instance, I am not sure whether someone who can read Augustine in Latin will understand the odes by Horace.

TANEDA: I am aware of the cultural significance of Latin, but not of its practical importance. Thus I decided that, as far as I am concerned, I would acquire only the basics of its grammar… In addition, I read *De Bello Gallico* [On the Gallic War] by Julius Caesar—in French translation—and a few works by Tacitus.[153]

DIENES: I am not in favor of teaching Latin. The results pupils normally achieved after eight years of study was out of proportion to the invested time and energy. It is often argued that Latin grammar sharpens the mind. The same is also claimed of math. Well, the Russian language sharpens it at least as much.

Latin is conducive to the acquisition of Romance languages, but these languages do not make use of Latin's complicated declensions. Use of the sequence of tenses—a bugbear of English

---

153. Author's note: I had some trouble understanding the name of Tacitus, as my Japanese friend pronounced his name "Takitousu." Here is how a "supranational" language is distorted to become national.

186 / HARMONY OF BABEL

language examinations—is not furthered by the knowledge of *consecutio temporum*. Latin does contribute to finding the right forms in Spanish...but is that worth adding many years of Latin study to the curricula?

I am enthusiastic about Esperanto because its grammar is minimal, and its methods of derivation are enhanced to the maximum. The only problem is that I do not know what to use it for.

BACK: They usually mention two benefits of Latin instruction. On the one hand, it is considered to be a school of thought *(Denkschule)*; on the other hand, it enriches one's native vocabulary. Even if I admit both its merits, I still feel it taxes the memory too much. So many rules—and at least as many exceptions! It is true that by becoming familiar with, say, the concept of *ablative absolute,* a new way opens to the realm of thinking, but one cannot utilize this piece of information in other languages.[154]

As far as Esperanto is concerned, I would be happy to see it spread as far and wide as possible. I envy my Hungarian neighbors because Esperanto even has a department at the University of Budapest, led by the distinguished Professor Szerdahelyi.[155] There is none in Vienna—but there is a special Esperanto section in the prestigious *Nationalbibliothek* (National Library). I find it a great advantage of the language that it allows free rein to derivation, in contrast to ethnic or national languages, in which word formation is hampered by prejudice or unconventionality. Concerning its

154. The ablative absolute is an event expressed as an element of the main clause by way of a nonfinite verb form (instead of using a full subordinate clause), cf. "His boss being away, he was less pressed for time." As shown by this example, the concept may be helpful in understanding modern languages.
155. Esperanto Language and Literature as a major was launched in 1966 at Eötvös Loránd University, Budapest.

future, I am unfortunately not optimistic.

D'ABADIE: The studies of a physician, a biologist, or a theologian are aided by a command of Latin, but the average person can do without it. It has not filled the role of a universal means of communication since the time it became an uprooted, "dead" language. Now they want to develop Esperanto into a world language, even though it has never been a "living" language.[156]

KÉPES: Latin is needed! It does not serve any communicative purposes? Well, that's too bad! We ought to speak Latin. Esperanto does not attract me; I have no intention to learn it.

POSSEMIERS: Latin is necessary because it facilitates learning all Romance languages. With its help I can even succeed in Romanian, as far as its Latinate vocabulary allows me.

FLIFLET: As far as I am concerned, I sincerely regret that in Greek I never got any further than reciting the Our Father. The fact that there is generally no Latin instruction seems to me a loss, but a cultural loss, not a practical one. However, I find Esperanto excellent exactly for practical reasons. Then again, I doubt it can become a world language. I am not even entirely sure if it will be suitable for the creation of literary works.[157]

Art springs from life: An internationally regulated language leaves little room for individual initiative. If a language wants to live, it must change. On the other hand, when it changes freely, it cannot play a universal role.

BERG: The dominant role of English cannot be denied. If

---

156. Esperanto is currently used; for this reason it qualifies as a living language.
157. Based on the *Concise Encyclopedia of the Original Literature of Esperanto* (728 pages), there is little doubt about it now. This corpus includes works by the Scottish poet William Auld, nominated for the Nobel Prize in Literature. Its translated literature boasts works by authors from Shakespeare to Tolkien.

we do want to have a common language, why would it not be that wonderfully flexible and, most of all, *brief* English? I consider Esperanto a dream—a beautiful dream.

The knowledge of Latin—or Greek—is dispensable. But let us not forget that living European languages were built on them! Therefore whoever wants to acquire several languages should be acquainted with the two classical tongues. This way one can discover that these many languages are, in fact, *one* language.

By the way, I am just now noticing that I omitted Latin from the list of my languages. It has the role of a mother language to me to such an extent that I do not even feel the need to mention it.

EGE: A supranational language has an initial disadvantage at its launch: that it stands above nations. Each country strives to assert itself and its language. It is a pity. Esperanto has made a big step forward: It surpassed even English in simplifying declension and conjugation.

GOLDEN: Regarding a common language, facts had decided the matter before linguists could arrive at a common denominator. At the moment, English fills this role. In my opinion, the dominance of English is not because of merits inherent in the language, but because of historical and economic circumstances. Its undeniable advantage is simplicity: According to Ogden and Richards (*Basic English*), almost every action can be expressed with *get* and *put* plus one of 16 other verbs. By the way, *Basic* does not mean "basic" but is an acronym of British American Scientific International Commercial.

Latin is important to those dealing with the humanities— especially linguists. But it also enables zoologists, botanists, and physicians to understand each other. We call it a dead language, although Latin (and Greek) prove their viability when we turn to them whenever we need to devise new words for new concepts.

As far as Esperanto is concerned, I would welcome its being taught in schools, not instead of national languages, but as a supplement to them. Of course, I do not know if a Chinese speaker, who does not use suffixation, would find Esperanto easier to cope with than a natural language. In my opinion, it was a pity to invent a special ending for the accusative, even if it provides greater flexibility in word order.

To my knowledge, there are currently eight million people speaking Esperanto. It is an impressive number, though just a drop in the ocean of the 400 million native speakers of English.

LOMB: I was excellent in Latin in high school; nowadays it takes me hours to translate an ode by Horace. I suppose everybody who graduated from a grammar school, except some classical scholars, does similarly or even worse.

"Jurists and physicians must study Latin" goes the argument of those who persist in its instruction.

If law students can grapple with the millions of rules and statutes in civil law, criminal law, international law, etc., they will also be able to acquire at university those handful of Latin terms that will be required in their judge's, lawyer's, or attorney's practice! As for the Latinate vocabulary of medicine, most of them are of Greek origin. A prospective *rheumatologist, psychiatrist, cardiologist, orthopedist,* or *dermatologist* will study the *symptoms, diagnosis,* and *therapy* of *asthma, thrombosis, epilepsy, paralysis,* and *trauma* in Greek. Yet no one in secondary schools demands that medical students learn Greek!

Concerning the worldwide spread of Esperanto: As an enthusiastic humanist, I am hopeful for it. As one who makes a living by interpreting, I am afraid of it. As a linguist, I wish it would react more flexibly to the simplifications that have taken place in living national languages in the past hundred-plus years.

Q: Are there "easy" and "difficult," "rich" and "poor," "beautiful" and "less beautiful" languages?

FLIFLET: Generally English is considered not only the most important language but also the easiest to acquire. However, my heart has always drawn me more to the east and the south. Hungarian and Finnish are closer to me than, for instance, Italian, though I admit that Dante's language rings more harmoniously. I even studied Italian—but it went slower than, for example, Dutch. Dutch is closer to my Norwegian mother tongue.

BACK: When learning Hungarian, I had a pleasant surprise: I realized that it obeys some rules that can be formulated clearly. In other words, it turned out that the language is *predictable:* If I, say, want to know a rule to form a noun from an adjective, I can usually find the noun in the dictionary.

The difficulty I have to overcome—just as other foreigners do, I suppose—is the position of verbal prefixes: *odamegyünk— megyünk oda* (we go there).[158] Beauty and ugliness are aesthetic concepts. As such, they cannot be judged objectively.

VON HABSBURG: An ugly language? I do not know of one. I like French because every word describes a specific and unambiguous concept. If I may resort to a metaphor, speaking English is like shooting a shotgun: You are bound to hit something. Whoever speaks French hunts with a rifle: The bullet will hit exactly on target. I could call French the language of the law. Let us

---

158. In Hungarian, grammatical and semantic factors determine whether a modifier is prefixed to the verb or written as a separate, postpositioned particle.

think of treaties, contracts, or agreements intended to protect the weaker party against the stronger one.

If the terms of a language are ambiguous—as in German—then the stronger party may make use of the inaccuracy and turn it as a weapon against the weaker one.

NAUMENKO: In terms of the difficulty of learning, there is no difference. Each language is equally difficult—or, if I want, equally easy. Usually pronunciation causes the most problems, but Russians generally speak foreign languages well. It is because in language training we attach much importance to phonetics.

MARTINET: You find a foreign language easier depending on how much you can appropriate from your native language knowledge. But there are objective criteria as well. I have seen, for instance, that the language knowledge of a Danish child at five satisfies his or her environment. The knowledge of a French preschool child at the same age is not yet considered acceptable. Does it mean that the Danish language is easier? No, it means that the French are more demanding.

Of course, acquiring writing skills is difficult in languages where the written form cannot be inferred from the pronounced form. To put it more academically, writing is more difficult where there is no or little correspondence between graphics and phonics.

Are there any poor and rich languages? It is definitely not possible to draw an inference from the thickness of dictionaries to the wealth of vocabulary! I would rather accept this: How many shades of a *single* concept can be expressed in a language?

Another criterion is how much of the existing vocabulary (in dictionaries) is actually used in real life. Needless to say, developing countries need to develop their own languages.

KÉPES: They organized a contest in Hungary in the thirties[159] to decide which is the most beautiful language. Estonian took the prize with this sentence: *Sõida tasa üle silla* (Drive slowly over the bridge). As for other languages, for me, there are too many consonants in Czech, and Italian is too soft.

There is no difficult language; each can be learned. I became familiar with Ancient Greek at 16; I resolved to acquire Modern Greek 40 years later. It went incredibly fast. Perhaps I found my way back to my youth.

GREEN: Yes, there are rich and poor languages. French is, for example, poor, difficult, and beautiful. It grew impoverished in the 17th century. Before that time, Rabelais and contemporary poets wrote lavishly. Then came a few gentlemen who "put it in order": Descartes, Boileau, and Malherbe. It is a regrettable fact, but it is amazing how much the French can still do with their language, which was squeezed into a narrow stream.

Sometimes I find delight in the ring of languages that I do not understand. An example, in your language, is when I listen to Bartók's *Bluebeard* in Hungarian.

There are small languages and dialects that are difficult to learn and unpleasant to the ear. But this is not why I call them small. I do so because they do not have genuine literatures.

A language gains inner light from great works. This light is what a great poet records—and culls at the same time. Of course, it is only the really great artists who are capable of doing so, the ones who compose poetry even if they happen to write in prose. French was further embellished by Saint-Simon, Baudelaire, and Claudel.

I find Russian really beautiful, and I love Italian. But how can

---

159. It may be an urban legend, at least concerning Hungary as its venue.

you not love something that comes from Italy?

SUGÁR: A difficult language? I considered German difficult. *Der, die, das*[160] cannot be understood with logic; they should be learned in childhood. German is not among my favorites even today, although I use it fairly often as a television correspondent.

PILCH: By the "beauty" of a language, we usually mean its richness reflected in literary works. Let us just recall masterworks of Celtic or French poetry! The more attractive the culture upon which a language was built, the more beautiful we find it.

FÉLIX: There are no easier or more difficult languages. The morphology of English is easy; however, its vowel system defeats all non-natives.

The beauty of a language is as difficult to formulate as that of a work of art. I find Danish, Dutch, and some tonal languages (that depend on pitch) less engaging. If I were to find some objective criterion, I would say that I like sonorous languages, which have a clear ring. Examples are Russian and Italian.

KING: One can speak about ease and difficulty only in a relative sense. If I replace the *-tion* ending of English nouns with *-ción,* I get a perfect Spanish word in the majority of cases. But Chinese people who do not speak English are not helped by this trick. Such devices took me nowhere when I was studying Arabic.

As far as beauty is concerned, a linguist ought not to make a statement about it. I feel it is a prejudice. One decides depending on one's culture what, for instance, true poetry must be like!

I do not consider the richness of vocabulary an important fac-

---

160. The three variants of the definite article "the" indicate gender in German. For example, *der Tisch* (the table) is masculine, *die Tür* (the door) is feminine, and *das Fenster* (the window) is neuter. However, endings of nouns and the forms of related articles and adjectives often provide some clue.

tor. My native English certainly uses a number of terms to name species of trees, but it has never disturbed me that I did not encounter this embarrassment of riches in another language.

TOULOUZE: I find beauty an entirely subjective category dependent on the approach of a speaker. But one cannot unambiguously classify languages as being easy or difficult to acquire: In one, you struggle with pronunciation; in another, you are stumped by syntax. I am especially allergic to this question, anyway, because Hungarian is trumpeted—not infrequently even by Hungarians—to be difficult to learn, thus stifling the interest to learn it, or even suppressing learning that has already begun.

The richness and poorness of languages should also be judged with more subtlety. In certain tongues, there is an impressive wealth of nouns; in others, you can praise (or curse) the diversity of verbs. Vocabulary is a consequence of the geographical location and the history of a people. "Primitive" peoples who use traditional means of production may not have exact terms for the features of urban life, but their vocabulary concerning fishing and hunting has outsmarted more than one French linguist and lexicographer.

BERG: The mystery of the beauty of a language lies in the heart of the person who speaks it.

KADA: Everybody considers his or her own mother tongue the most beautiful. I, of course, prefer Hungarian. *Amor sanctus* [a translation of medieval Latin hymns into Hungarian by Mihály Babits, 1933] is a magnificent work. There are quite a few artists of language among our contemporary authors as well.

As far as the richness and poorness of languages is concerned, a language is poorer if its speakers live in a relatively undeveloped region (perhaps hampered by historical factors).

D'ABADIE: For an Englishman, every language is difficult.

The reason is not because they are untalented, but because motivation is lacking: People around the world strive to make themselves understood in English. What's more, a complex grammar is unfamiliar to English speakers. To their minds, it is the idiomatic connection of words, rather than suffixes of inflection and derivation, that conveys the meaning of speech. French people's ignorance of foreign languages is explained by their chauvinism. They cannot forget that diplomats from around the world once used to negotiate in their language.

GOLDEN: No one is free of bias: One's mother tongue is closer to one's heart. Yet each language consists of sounds, and there is no denying that certain sounds are pleasing, and others are dissonant. Of course, our perception of the culture behind a language may influence our opinion of whether it sounds pleasing or not.

German is harder simply due to its sound clusters; I mean words such as *trug* (he/she carried). It surely does not sound pleasant from the mouth of a miner from the Ruhr region. Italian is melodious (it uses many vowels), but I heard fisherwomen quarreling at a Palermo market—well, it was not a catchy tune. The Hawaiian language sounds ingratiating. It consists of five vowels and merely eight consonants.

A "difficult" language? Naturally, one should ask *to whom* is it difficult. In Ireland, Irish is one of the official languages. If someone hears only Irish at home, he or she will have more difficulty with English lessons in school. English is spoken by 97% of the population of the British Isles.

Generally speaking, Spanish is counted among the easy languages, but for the Basque who live in Spain, it is no easier than, say, German or another foreign tongue.

LOMB: For a Pole, Russian is easy, and Italian is difficult.[161] As for Germans, they can learn Swedish and Norwegian standing on their heads.

Last November I was compelled by the cold to enter a café on the outskirts of Oslo. All I had to feast my eyes on were local papers. By the time I received and drank my tea, I had read and understood everything, from the editorial through the small ads, thanks to my rather mediocre command of Swedish.

If we set this specific "ease" aside, which depends on the knowledge of a student, we can try to establish objective criteria. We can determine, for example, if there are phenomena in the given tongue that cannot be understood logically. Perhaps there are features that follow so many rules (and exceptions to these rules) that it is simpler to learn the right form blindly. To my mind, difficult rules include, for example, definite and indefinite conjugations in Hungarian,[162] perfective and imperfective forms[163] of verbs in Russian, the whimsical connection between writing and sound in English, and *der, die,* and *das* in German.

Despite the general view of my interviewees, I dare say there exists a most difficult language in the absolute sense: Japanese.[164] I have more trouble with it than with all the others combined.

The reason isn't symbols; studying them is amusing and in-

---

161. Linguistically, "for a Pole, Slovak is easy, and French is difficult" would be a more justifiable statement.
162. E.g., definite conjugation: I see *the* tree. – Lát*om a* fát. Indefinite conjugation: I see *a* tree. – Lát*ok egy* fát.
163. Cf. "entered" and "was entering" in English.
164. The Foreign Service Institute (FSI) of the U.S. Department of State and the National Virtual Translation Center mention Arabic, Cantonese and Mandarin Chinese, Japanese, and Korean as "exceptionally difficult for native English speakers"; the first organization names Japanese as more difficult than the others, but the latter specifies Korean.

triguing. The problem is the many homophones (words with the same sound but a different meaning) and synonyms (words with a different sound but the same meaning)!

For example, I have found nine synonyms for the verb "study": *manabu, narau, oboeru, kenkyu suru, shutoku suru, gakushu suru, keiko suru, masuta* (master) *suru,* and *benkyo suru.*[165]

Japanese people's associations of ideas, quite unlike those of European people, also render it more difficult to find out the meaning of a word. I soon realized that *furiko* (literally, "the child of swinging") simply means *pendulum.* But it was harder to figure out that whoever wants to buy talcum powder should ask for *ase-shirazu*—that is, a box of "ignorant of perspiration."

At the same time, *jishin* means the hour hand, self-confidence, an earthquake, a magnetic needle, and oneself. On the other hand, *sanka* can equally be a disaster, a song of praise, oxidation, obstetrics, participation, and a subsidiary. Of course, the written form is different for each, and you can guess from the context which your partner happens to mean at the moment. But if they suddenly change topic, and if the context gives no "prompt," I am just as lost as when someone unexpectedly asks me on the street, "Would you please help me get to *Petőfi* Street?" (Ten of them are registered in the postal code listing for Budapest, apart from four more *Petőfi Sándor* Streets.)

Which is the most beautiful language? For me, it is always the one that I am currently reading or speaking, except for my mother tongue. Unfortunately, because in Hungarian the stress always comes on the first syllable, foreigners often do not find it beautiful. "Each new word gives another knock on my brain," a

---

165. Only the first three are originally verbs.

tactless French person once said to me. "And those many *e* sounds! Just like a goat bleating."

I dared not quote our Petőfi:

"*Mely nyelv merne versenyezni véled?*"[166]

Q: What is multilingualism good for?

> The various languages you ought to have: One for your mother, which you will subsequently never speak again; one which you only read but never dare to write; one in which you pray but without understanding a single word; one in which you do arithmetic and to which all money matters belong; one in which you write (but no letters); one in which you travel, and in this one you can also write your letters. And finally, there is a language in which you write your works—that is, those few who ever write.[167]
>
> —Elias Canetti, Nobel Prize laureate, 1981

These lines have a quiet melancholy. Canetti, an expert in multilingualism, was born to parents who had escaped from Spain. He spent time in Ruse, Bulgaria, where "On any one day you could hear seven or eight languages." The city of Giurgiu, adjacent to Ruse, is entirely Romanian. His parents spoke German to each other; the children, Spanish; the nursemaid, only Bulgarian.

He was taken to England in his primary school years, and though he hardly knew the language, he read the *Arabian Nights,* the *One Thousand and One Nights.* England was where he began learning French, "or rather, its Manchester version."

I asked my interviewees what they thought multilingualism

---

166. "[O Nature, glorious Nature,] who would dare / with reckless tongue to match your wondrous fare?" From "The Tisza," translated by Watson Kirkconnel.
167. From *The Human Province* (except for the last sentence; source is unknown)

was good for.

POSSEMIERS: If you are an interpreter, it is good for nothing. You have to deal with your selected main language so much that you have no time to use other languages. And even then you cannot keep up with the constant increase of vocabulary in your main language! Learning new phrases, using them properly and at the right time—it is difficult enough in one language alone. In our profession, it actually breeds distrust when someone speaks too many languages. Tell me, what would you think of a medicine that is equally recommended for shingles, an inflamed throat, loss of hair, and a peptic ulcer?

GOLDEN: Financially speaking, the command of multiple languages does not mean very much in my country. But learning them is an inexhaustible source of joy and a means of self-realization. Becoming familiar with a new language, for me, is not only an intellectual thrill and an emotional satisfaction, but an almost physical happiness.

VON HABSBURG: You can get to know and understand every nation best through its language. It is words that connect people with one another. Although the most polyglot person in Strasbourg is a British MEP[168] named Battersby,[169] who speaks seven languages, including Hungarian, multilinguals are very rare among Britons and Americans. They can fare very well between the Atlantic and the Pacific Ocean with their native tongue. However, the lack of language skills is a big disadvantage in foreign trade. Regardless of whether they make good-quality products, monolingual businesses have difficulty entering foreign markets; they have difficulty adjusting themselves to the mindsets of pro-

168. Member of the European Parliament.
169. Robert Christopher Battersby (1924–2002).

spective customers. They do badly in the psychology of sales and marketing.

KÉPES: A great advantage of polyglottism is that you can access many pieces of literature first-hand. A disadvantage is that whoever is labeled as a polyglot will be underrated as an author. Maybe truly brilliant geniuses should speak only one language; then they would be sooner acknowledged as creative talents.

FLIFLET: I have never had a goal in sight: I pleased myself by learning. But it was my language skills that allowed me to make contacts and find good friends in several countries in Europe. How good it felt, for example, right after the 1914–1918 world war, to be able to speak with the Austrian and German *Hungerkinder* (starving children) who were invited to be fed in Norway!

GREEN: I can put it down to my dual mother tongues that I can enjoy French and English poetry to the exact same degree. Villon, Baudelaire, and Rimbaud are equal to Keats. But first of all is Shakespeare. When I read his dramas for the first time, I cried with joy.

BACK: My job—directing the administration of the Interpreting School in Vienna—requires me to deal with multiple languages. I consider multilingualism counterproductive from the point of view of quality. To use a primitive metaphor: If a cat chases 10 mice at once, it will catch fewer than by chasing only one.

D'ABADIE: Whoever likes traveling will find language skills the most valuable key; it helps open the locks of countries, habits, people, and traditions. What complements this experience is understanding the local radio and television programs.

I also get to know more about my own homeland if I speak other languages. I tend to read French papers in London and English papers in Paris. They inform me more than those published at home. For instance, I learned from French papers that mutton had to be banned in South Wales as the result of nuclear leakage. English papers told the story only with euphemisms.

DIENES: In my opinion, it is not worth knowing more than two languages "actively." But learning them—at least for me—is endless pleasure, play, and amusement.

NAUMENKO: I would suggest to all those who do not work specifically as a linguist by trade that they should acquire one world language apart from their mother tongue, and they should also have a special (outsider) language.

KADA: I very much regret that I know no Slavic languages. I have always intended to learn one—I just haven't had the time.

SUGÁR: In my profession, language skills are worth gold. I have reported in 80 countries, and I do interviews in 10 languages. I am motivated by an interest in people, by a desire to make friends, by a sense of achievement, and—I confess—by some exhibitionist tendencies.

By the way, I know of only one pleasure greater than the command of languages: learning them.

DEAR READERS: The following question must have been presented to all of my polyglot colleagues over the years:

Q: Don't the languages get mixed up in your head?

I asked them the question as well.

First I will quote the most competent one, Mezzofanti—based on the answer he gave to an amazed contemporary: "Have you ever tried on a pair of green spectacles?…While you wore these spectacles, everything was green to your eyes. It is precisely

202 / HARMONY OF BABEL

so with me. While I am speaking a [foreign] language, for instance Russian, I put on my Russian spectacles, and for the time being, they color everything Russian. I see all my ideas in that language alone. If I change to another language, I have changed my spectacles again, and it is the same for that language too!"

DIENES: It occurred to me once that I jumbled up languages: Swedish and Italian. Upon reflection, I found that I had attained the same level of knowledge in them: I forgot Swedish commensurate to the level I learned Italian (and vice versa), and that was how they got to the same arena.

KEMÉNY: I do not confuse languages.

TANEDA: Let me quote my mother tongue. When it borrows words from another language (of course, usually from English), it "Japanizes" them, adapting them to its own structure and pronunciation. That is how, for example, *world series* becomes *wurudu sirizu*. When I weave these words into a Japanese text, I also pronounce them in the exact same (Japanese) way. But when I switch to English, I pull down the "window" of my mother tongue, I pull up that of English, and in this new context the Japanized form does not even come into my mind.

I find good pronunciation decisive in this regard. If the "tune" is correct, the melody will guide you to the right way and protect you from being derailed.

SUGÁR: After spending two weeks in a Spanish-speaking region, I actually have to be careful when switching to Italian not to mingle Spanish words into my speech. At the same time, I never muddle up Slavic languages. Why? I have no idea.

KÉPES: If I set the floor lamp to a given point, it will illuminate only a definite area, and the rest will stay in the dark. I never confuse Slavic languages.

LOMB: I confuse languages at times, mostly those that I speak less frequently. When we were trying to find criteria for assessing language skill, we could have accepted as one criterion how much time is needed to switch between languages.

Concerning my main languages, this switch takes a few minutes; in languages in which I have less practice, a few hours; in those I rarely use, a few days.

Naturally, the risk of confusion is especially high for languages of the same family. The similarity of Spanish and Italian causes me so much trouble that once, in frustration, I translated a two-page-long text into both languages, and I wrote the two versions in my notebook next to each other. It helped.

It is an extra annoyance for me that the Italian *si* (impersonal subject or reflexive object) is *se* in Spanish, and the Italian *se* (if) is *si* in Spanish. However, both of them are written *se* and pronounced *si* in Portuguese. Paradoxically, it may be complications like these that make learning languages colorful, joyful, and worthwhile.

I reject the commonplace that you are worth as many people as the languages you speak. Folly remains folly even if someone happens to repeat it in 10 languages. But I believe and profess that the more languages you speak, the more interesting and authentic image you have of the world. You also gain a better picture of the one person who is personally most exciting: *your own self.*

Multilingualism is appraised differently in different parts of the world. In Scandinavian countries, it is considered natural: Schoolchildren, conductors, and shop assistants will answer your questions with a fair command of English. In England, multilingualism is considered an odd pastime like collecting butterflies or breeding pigeons. The English do not have high standards; the recognition *He is a good linguist* applies to anybody who can stumble out a sentence.

In my country, as the deformations of the fifties[170] are gone, it is considered more necessary (and I hope it will soon be taken for granted) to have a mastery of one or two foreign languages.

But I cannot resist trying to entertain the dear reader by relating two of my personal experiences.

Many people have asked me how I could deal with learning Russian in the midst of the horrors of war. I keep answering: It was just this learning that helped me endure the cold, the hunger, the fear of being found out, and the anxiety about the future.[171]

With the siege raging, I tried to pass the time in the dark cellar by constantly working on the conversation I would have with the first Russian soldier who set foot in it. I decided to embellish each sentence with a few adjectival and adverbial participles (my mastery of these was the shakiest). Moreover, I would dazzle him not only with the ease and elegance of my command of his language, but with my literary accomplishments as well: I would draw parallels between the poetry of Pushkin and Lermontov; I would sing the praises of Sholokhov's epic style; and so on and so forth.

That was the dream. The reality, in contrast, was that in the sudden quiet of the dawning New Year's Day, I stole up into the bleak and barren garden surrounding the building. Barely had I

---

170. Probably the dictatorship (lasting until 1956) under Mátyás Rákosi, who allegedly called himself Stalin's best pupil.
171. The following paragraphs are from Lomb's first book, *Polyglot: How I Learn Languages*, pp. 27–28.

filled my lungs with a few fresh breaths when a rather young soldier jumped over the fence into the garden. He was clutching a milk jug, making it obvious what he was doing there. But he did utter a few words:

"Korova est?" he asked.

I, on the other hand, was so discombobulated with excitement that I didn't even recognize the word for "cow." The young man tried to help.

"Korova! You know? Moo...oo...oo!"

As I just kept staring at him agape, he shrugged and jumped over the other fence.

The second encounter happened a few hours later, by which time I had had a chance to get over the first fiasco.

This time a very young man opened the door of the cellar. He asked for salt, then took some bread and bacon out of his rucksack and set to eating comfortably, every once in a while offering us a bite on the point of his jack-knife. When he realized that I spoke Russian, he was greatly moved.

"Molodets Partisanka!" (Well done, little guerrilla!) He shook my hand vigorously.

After a while, some Romanian officers entered. (We were liberated at Rákosfalva, where Romanian troops were also stationed.)

"What kind of language are you speaking with those guys?" The Russian soldier said, scowling.

"I'm speaking French," I replied.

The young Russian shook his head, then packed up his provisions, stood up, and started out. From the threshold, he hissed back at me: *"Shpionka!"* (Little spy!)

So much for being multilingual!

Why Is Language Instruction Ailing in Hungary?

≈

POLITELY SPEAKING, I would phrase the question like this: How effective is language learning in Hungary? Politely speaking, I would answer, "Not very."

If we were to express its efficiency in terms of mathematics, some kind of fraction should be used. Its denominator would consist of the number of people who *study* a particular language, and its numerator, people who *speak* that language.

As for the denominator, we can approximate it. I could not obtain comprehensive statistical data, but foreign language education is included in the curriculum of all our primary and secondary schools, universities, and colleges. There is a legion of clubs, language schools, and business partnerships that advertise themselves in daily newspapers, offering learning opportunities with a looser or tighter schedule. Many qualified educators give private lessons, and a considerable number of young people and adults learn on their own.

The numerator of the fraction, however—the number who

speak the language—cannot even be estimated. On the one hand—as it has been mentioned several times—to "know" a language is ambiguous. Even if we devised some generally accepted unit to rate language knowledge (like *pascal* for pressure or *joule* for energy), we could not measure it. We would not have any international criteria at our disposal other than the self-assessment on survey questionnaires. It is a subjective and unreliable piece of data.

In any case, you don't need an objective survey to know that my compatriots' language skills are not sufficient; I can inform you from sad experience. In our country, strangers are received with a grin and a puzzled scratching of the ear even by those who meet them most frequently: cab drivers, bus inspectors, policemen, and downtown shop assistants. This is an especially painful fact if we consider that the tourists who visit Hungary do not bring along a key to open up the lock of our language.

I am aware that I am quoting a commonplace. Let me redeem myself by trying to locate some of the reasons for this countrywide ignorance. Reasons that I have already described several times and that can be found by anyone interested in this question are as follows:

1. Institutions and schools generally cannot provide the concentrated instruction required for the well-paced acquisition of a language. My own language-learning method (which has little to do with the topic of this book) recommends many exercises to be done on one's own.

2. The small number of classes and the large number of pupils do not make it possible for education to be centered on the student. The aim of language instruction is to teach how to *com-*

municate. Every act of communication has two main characters: *I,* the one speaking, and *you,* the one addressed. Yet lessons in books—especially the old ones—are still commonly phrased in the third person.

Books certainly describe in impeccable English that Mr. Smith is reading a paper in an armchair while Mrs. Smith is setting the table. But it takes you a long time to develop the ability to answer your foreign partner's inquiry and ask for what you want.

(Again: It is the reading of books that appeal to your own interests rather than studying a course book, keeping a diary, and talking to yourself that can help you compose a message concerning the most interesting person—your own self.)

3. Yes, the message! Prehistoric man did not become human when he climbed down from the trees and stood on two legs. Rather, it was when he realized that bringing down a prehistoric buffalo was easier in a group than beating it to death with a piece of rock on his own. For this purpose he created the means of communication, a wonderful achievement of the human species: language.

It is the strain to communicate that prompts you to descend onto the sinking, shaky ground of a foreign language.

The benefits of living abroad are generally overrated. The interaction between a tourist and a native is usually a sentence or two. Yet the motivation is tangible. Touring urges you to start speaking, even if you are stuttering, stammering, and blushing in advance about your mistakes: "Is there a pair of shoes one size bigger than these?" "From which track does the evening express leave?"

Between a teacher and his or her students, no necessary strain of communication arises. Classes are short, and the difference between pupils' knowledge is wide. What's more, the teacher's effort to create lifelike situations is usually contrived.

4. Understanding and producing a foreign language is educated guesswork.

You cannot stop marveling that a child can construct an unlimited variety of forms from a limited number of known facts. The same is true for an adult using a foreign language. *Construction is through trial and error.* However, although each failed attempt by a little child at coining a word or making a sentence is rewarded by the parents with a rapturous smile, a pupil is punished with a reprimand and a bad mark.

A renowned educator was giving a high school junior an oral test in my presence. The girl wove into the recited lesson an expression that would have been logical based on the rules of the language—but the expression happened not to exist. The teacher, instead of appreciating the attempt, ridiculed her before the class for her "innovative approach" to language. The sense of failure, I am afraid, will stop the student short in her efforts to speak the language in the real world, outside the classroom.

Ironically, it is this guesswork that makes crossword puzzles popular across the country. Whoever travels by train can see in practically every compartment a white-headed pensioner, a tousled teenager, a soldier on leave, or a bureaucrat (bored with his documents) all bent over working on crosswords. Sucking their pencils, they rack their minds for what the answer could be for Roman goddess of beauty, five letters, horizontal.

Not for the world would they invest the same energy into another intellectual activity: guessing the meaning of unknown foreign words, verifying their dawning ideas, and discovering grammar rules autonomously.

Yet the two kinds of mental exercises are similar. A successful solution here and there brings the same joy of satisfaction to the mind: release after mild tension, a convergence of thoughts that started from different directions, and the practical creative joy of making order out of disorder.

5. What do we do when we start speaking in a foreign language? We try to be adroit. We instinctively avoid words we are not sure of and grammatical forms that may not be appropriate. We make compromises, we paraphrase, and we mimic. The school should not discredit these acts of adroitness.

Sometimes I even catch myself red-handed at this kind of subconscious manipulation of languages. I do so not only in the nerve-racking tension of simultaneous interpreting, but also during everyday conversations. I resign myself to the phrase that comes immediately to mind, even if I feel there is a more perfect word. I simplify when I become worried about some fairly complex grammatical form.

For example, I say *je vais m'asseoir* (I will sit down) in French instead of *je m'assoirai*. Or *nous venons d'obtenir* (we obtained) to avoid *nous obtînmes*. That is, I use the stable, unconjugated infinitive combined with a basic verb. I have to learn the infinitive anyway, and it is usable in a number of situations.

Of course, there is a shade of difference between these forms. Corneille and Racine may be turning in their graves, but my partner will certainly understand my phrases: The bridge of communication has been built.

Let me quote a Russian example. Russian is the mandato-

ry foreign language in Hungary.[172] It is also the first language I
learned consciously (and my favorite to this day).

I heard the complaint from Soviet tourists more than once
that it was impossible to get an answer from passersby even to
simple questions, such as "Which way is the museum?" The excellent language educator Madame Nelli Zhuravlyova teaches us in a
nice poem how to avoid the pitfalls of conjugations by employing
можно (mozhno; "can") and надо (nado; "must"), or how to rely
on the redeeming nonfinite forms. I tried to render some of the
poem's stanzas below:

Would you *care to* go to the Opera?
You *should* best take a taxi.
The performance *is* beginn*ing*.
You *ought to* hurry. Enjoy yourselves.

To the pharmacy? Beyond the tracks.
Look there! Straight ahead.
It is a large building with several stories.
You *can* almost see it from here.

If you *wish to* get to the park,
please turn right at the corner.
You are welcome, no problem,
It was my pleasure *to* help you.

Where is the suburban railway station?
You *don't need to* know much *to* find it.

---

172. Between 1949 and 1989.

Ten or twenty sentences, some data…
and a little bit of good will.[173]

—*Russian Conversation for Schoolchildren,* Tamara Szacski and
Nelli Zsuravljova (1988)

It would not hurt to call our pupils' attention to these opportunities for simplification. Or at least we can excuse them if they find out by themselves the easy ways offered by *Basic English* or *Basic Russian,* and if they make use of them.

Language is not mathematics! An equation can be solved only if you substitute the one and only correct value into all its terms. A linguistic "equation"—a sentence—will work even if you are not 100% precise. In scientific truths, mistakes are critical, but in language, all we risk is an F mark. Let those devoted to precision correct mistakes, but let teachers forgive us our trespasses, just as language will also certainly forgive those who trespass against it.

6. Institutional language instruction does not inspire self-instruction. It does not have room for anything but transmitting and testing knowledge.

Hard-working students can come to terms with the monotony of passive classroom learning. Their sense of duty helps them through the boredom of school.

---

173. The translator has italicized auxiliaries and other ways of working around conjugations. The original: "(…) Что прохожий хочет знать? / Где билеты покупать, / Как пройти и как проехать, / Где театр и где аптека, / Далеко ли до музея, / Как туда попасть быстрее? / На трамвае? На каком? / Может, можно и пешком? // Чтоб помочь найти дорогу, / Надо знать не очень много. / Если знаем сотню слов, / Наш ответ всегда готов. // — До угла идите прямо, / Надо там свернуть направо / И квартал пройти вперёд — / Там подземный переход (…)"

Question: Has anyone met a child who needed encouragement to play? A three-year-old runs tirelessly up and down the stairs and climbs every fence post. Why are they willing to play tag and hide-and-go-seek until complete exhaustion? Obviously, they are not led by the goal. They are not afraid of being found, caught, and captured. No, a playing child enjoys the process itself.

Each moment of running away, climbing up a hill, and hiding means testing and proving one's skills.

Learning a language can be similarly effective if it involves mental exercise and intellectual challenge. For example, if you discover a grammatical relationship in a language yourself, you can ascertain the meaning of a word/construction from its context and do not need to consult a dictionary or grammar book. Success justifies you: You deserve silent self-recognition, a bit of self-congratulation. Such an experience gives you motivation to go on with learning. Learning will be less tiring and happier, depending on how much of a role *homo ludens* (the Playing Man) will have in it, as opposed to *homo sapiens* (the Knowing Man).

I read an interesting piece of data recently in the 1985 yearbook of the American Psychological Association. There are many immigrant workers in the U.S., members of ethnic minorities. For their children, English is but a second language. Surprisingly, the survey found vast differences in the linguistic progress of children depending on whether they had come to the U.S. at the age of five or six. The variance cannot be explained by the age difference, the author of the article noted. Instead, the point was that the six-year-olds became familiar with the new language in school, while the younger ones learned it on the streets and in playgrounds—that is, in the open, cheerful, and stress-free atmosphere of playing. Children learn best when it is not the grade that is at stake but a question of who can run faster, hit the goal better, and come out on top in wrestling. Language learning is not the end but merely a means. I could even say that learning is a by-product.

It may be the superiority of language as a by-product that accounts for the success of schools [in Hungary] where some subjects—chemistry, physics, and biology—are taught in Russian, English, or German. The language itself becomes a kind of natural vehicle; the inhibitions involved in its acquisition loosen. It is fortunate that Hungary has more and more such schools.

How can the glum process of learning be transformed into an amusing mental exercise? I will try to explain with a simple practical example. Let us suppose that you are translating into French and you become unsure about a word. I suggest that your first resort should not be an English–French dictionary. The information you receive is just mechanically registered and—lacking any emotional-affective background—quickly forgotten. Why don't you try using a French–English (or monolingual) dictionary instead, and find out if the scrap of memory glimmering in your mind was correct? If so, the sense of achievement will hammer the expression into your brain permanently. If not, then…well and what of it![174]

A child plays tirelessly, and an adult spares no time and energy to pursue a current hobby. Adults play chess, hunt, ski, garden; these hobbies give them the opportunity to prove their own intellectual or physical capacities. Learning can also seem like distributing chocolate if you can attribute your new knowledge to your being smart and clever.

This experience can motivate you as effectively as any other

---

174. This phrase is given in English in the original, along with its Hungarian translation: *na bumm!*

reason that prompts you to learn languages (because Aunt Mary invited you to Paris, because technical literature is available only in German, because Yugoslavia is on the coast, or because there is more snow in Czechoslovakia, and you want to go there by car). We need success, that prerequisite for joyful learning and overcoming obstacles.

Language difficulties present themselves variously. There are languages, such as German, in which the difficulties are concentrated at the beginning of study. While studying the agreement of a variety of suffixes, you may have the impression that you are wandering in a pathless, dense forest. In the case of English, success shows up earlier. You can practically coax basic words into sentences.

With Russian, the novelty begins with the learning of letters. Interestingly, our school children generally find it more entertaining than deterring. They usually encounter the language in their early teenage years, when they start turning from a nice and kind child into a troubled adolescent. They find Cyrillic script a sort of ciphertext; it creates an island for them that is both in the world of youth but apart from adults, among whom they have not yet found their places.

When they reach the level of words, teenagers become unsure. Agglutinating and fusional languages are almost always more difficult. Teenagers also become perplexed by the unparalleled wealth of Russian vocabulary. "It is impossible to learn Russian," a friend of mine complained. "Every verb can begin with *pri, pre,* or *pro.*"

And what about English later on? It is not until weeks and months later that it dawns on you that it is far from simple.

Reaching the level of sentences and texts, we learn how natives actually express themselves. Unfortunately, often they do not speak in a way that you imagined based on the rules. A language consultant's red pencil will mercilessly plow through one's sentences formulated according to the instructions.

In his Ph.D. thesis, Dr. Miklós Eördögh demonstrated how in one of his novels Galsworthy broke rules for tense and verb forms rules. The Nobel laureate writer is lucky not to have applied for a state English examination in Hungary. He would have been ruthlessly flunked.

7. Returning to institutional language instruction: We cannot get rid of the burden of Latin instruction, which has traditionally looked at the study of language as the study of grammar. Yet language is both more than grammar and different from grammar. I would rather compare grammar to a kind of code.

Let us imagine a rather primitive cipher in diplomacy that requires, say, each letter "o" of the original text to be read as "ue," or each letter "b" as "v." Perhaps the "e" endings appear in code as "a." For similar languages, such an attempt may even lead to some success—it is called transfer or extrapolation.

For instance:

Italian	*Spanish*	
p*o*rto	p*ue*rto	(port, harbor)
p*o*nte	p*ue*nte	(bridge)
c*o*rda	c*ue*rda	(rope, string, cord)

German	*Dutch*	
le*b*en	le*v*en	(to live)
ge*b*en	ge*v*en	(to give)
kle*b*en	kle*v*en	(to stick)

English	Swedish
bite	bita
have	hava
ride	rida

Of course, we know what nonsense this mechanical conversion leads to in practice. But it is worth directing one's attention to it to remind ourselves that it exists.

Instead of such conversions, we teach grammar; what is more, we teach it in such a way that complicates self-evident things to the point of incomprehension even in the mother tongue. The result for students is antipathy toward learning *all* languages.

Teachers must cover the accusative case if only to make Hungarian pupils aware that its suffix can never be -*tt*.[175] However, I do not understand why children have to learn from their elementary school grammar books that "an action can be directed only toward those existing independent of the action: what is and was there before the onset of the action," whereas (a) the "object of result" must be distinguished from (b) the "object of direction."

To illuminate the difference between them, a certain textbook cites examples in two columns:

(a)	(b)
He is making a shoe.	He is mending a shoe.
She is baking a roll.	She is eating a roll.

I admit that I did not feel the difference. I can only hope that

---

175. The accusative suffix is always -*t* in Hungarian, sometimes preceded by a vowel. Some confuse the accusative with the ending of the past tense, which can be -*t* or -*tt*, often with a linking vowel, too.

12-year-olds have a linguistic culture surpassing mine and react to these theoretical shadings with more sensitivity. How those children who do not like reading (i.e., they cannot read) can be trained to love books is another issue. But this is certainly *not* the way to do so.

Let me grieve my heart with a quotation:

"Adapted from the Soviet People's Commissar Lunacharsky, some of our enthusiastic left-wing intelligentsia dreamed in 1946–1947 that apprentices should have a Latin volume of Catullus's poetry in their pockets in order to peruse it during the lunch break. Peasants would turn the pages of Virgil's *Georgicon* in the evenings…excusing them in advance for occasionally having to consult the dictionary for one or two unknown words" (György Sebestyén).

By contrast, we are happy if our youth are willing to browse comic strips, even if the appeal of comics does not lie in their having pictures but in having few letters. After all, Uncle Bob and his family members will, at most, plop down in front of the TV in the evenings to see the current crime story.

However, let me comfort my heart with another quotation:

"Words are gradually displaced by sights." Why is it comforting? Because it was noted more than a century ago, in 1880, by the since-forgotten Hungarian journalist Waldy.

Returning to institutional language instruction, it is a commonplace that learning is invariably uphill work, clambering up a steep slope. Its stages are fatigue, boredom, and occasional despair.

The way upward, of course, is not a constantly ascending slope. It more resembles a mountainside carved into terraces. More and more recent pieces of knowledge stack above each other periodically. Upon reaching a plateau, sometimes you have the impression that you have arrived, and you get your breath back. Then you realize that there are more steep rises above you. "I feel I have the hang of German at last," I boasted to a friend after studying it for a few years. "You are going to feel that quite a few more times," she said, casting a chill on my enthusiasm.

It is another commonplace that going uphill requires an engine and fuel—motivation. However, our course books often forget that even an engine in the best condition, or gasoline with the most favorable octane rating, may not function if you forget the lubricant. Although oil does not participate in the pulling, it enables for the smooth operation of the parts.

Textbooks roll out beautifully formed and well-rounded sentences before you. Your teachers demand that subject and predicate, and modifier and modified word, follow each other in flawless form. Teachers demand order in your speech, too. Something is still missing from sentences constructed in this manner, however. The machinery is creaking: You have forgotten the lubricant, the filler words of natural speech.

To close my book, I present some fillers from a short story by a contemporary Hungarian writer. I read the story to count the lubricating words, so to speak. I was surprised at the result. The author used an average of 11 fillers every 20 lines.

"Of course..." "since..." "I think..." "however..." "perhaps..." "then..." "but..." "yet..." "although..." "needless to say..." "as..." "besides..." "nevertheless..." "naturally..." "after all..." The fillers did not sound superfluous at all, spaced judiciously throughout the text as they were. I would not even have noticed them had I not set out to nitpick deliberately.

It will be helpful if you store these terms in your memory; they lubricate and accent everyday speech. You can cling to them until your brain is ready to compose your actual message. I mean phrases such as "I also have to say that..." "The fact is that..." "It reminds me..." "I would like to note that..." I have never anywhere encountered a textbook that included such expressions, which are frequent in conversation.

Also missing is that life-saving phrase you will certainly need the first time you are addressed in a foreign language:

"I'm sorry?"

Selected References

Annenkov, P. V. (1960). *Literaturnye vospominaniya.* (n.p.).

Canetti, E. (1978). *The human province.* Trans. J. Neugroschel. New York: Seabury Press.

Darmesteter, A. (1886). *The life of words as the symbols of ideas.* London: Kegan Paul, Trench & Co.

Duka, T. (1885). *Life and works of Alexander Csoma de Körösi.* London: Trübner & Co. Ludgate Hill.

Green, J. (1985). *The language and its shadow.* Paris: Éditions de la Différence.

Haas, G. (1992). *Európáért. Haas György beszélgetései Dr. Habsburg Ottóval* [György Haas's conversations with Dr. Otto von Habsburg]. Békéscsaba: Tevan.

Headley, J. T. (1845). *Letters from Italy.* New York and London: Wiley and Putnam.

Jókai, Mór. (1872). *Eppur si muove—És mégis mozog a Föld* [And yet it moves]. (n.p.).

Kemény, F. (1975). *Das Sprechenlernen der Völker* [Speech learning of nations]. Wien: Wilhelm Braumüller.

Keesing, F. A. G. (1939). *Het Evenwichtsbegrip in de Economische Literatuur* [The Concept of Equilibrium in Economic Literature]. Purmerend: J. Muusses.

Lénard, A. S. (1969). *Római történetek* [Roman stories]. Budapest: Magvető.

Lomb, K. (2008, 2011). *Polyglot: How I learn languages.* Trans. K. DeKorne & Á. Szegi. Berkeley, CA: TESL-EJ Publications.

Lomb, K. (2016). *With languages in mind: Musings of a polyglot.* Trans. Á. Szegi. Berkeley, CA: TESL-EJ Publications.

Lomonosov, M. V. (1757). Предисловие о пользе книг церковных в российском языке [Preface on the benefits of church books in the Russian language]. In: Полное собрание сочинений [Complete works] (1952). Vol. VII, pp. 585–592. Moscow–Leningrad: Издательство Академии Наук СССР [Publishing house of the Academy of Sciences of the USSR]. Quoted in: Misley, P. and Gazda, I. Jr. (Eds.).

Misley, P. & Gazda, I. Jr. (Eds.) (1982). *Mihail Lomonoszov válogatott írásai* [Selected writings of M. Lomonosov]. Budapest: Helikon–Európa.

Pinker, S. (1994, January 29). Grammar puss. *The New Republic.* Retrieved from https://newrepublic.com

Pliny the Elder. *Natural History*, 7.25. http://perseus.uchicago.edu/

Plutarch. (1823). *Plutarch's Lives.* Translated by J. and W. Langhorne. London. (n.p.).

Prideaux. (1808). *Life of Mahomet.* London: (n.p.).

Pulszky, F. (1958). *Életem és korom* [My life and times]. Budapest: Szépirodalmi Könyvkiadó. (Original edition 1880–82).

Russell, C. W. (1858). *The life of Cardinal Mezzofanti, with an introductory memoir of eminent linguists, ancient and modern.* London: Longman.

Sarbu, A. (1974). *Joseph Conrad világa* [Joseph Conrad's World]. Budapest: Európa.

Schliemann, H. (1881). *Ilios, the city and country of the Trojans…including an autobiography of the author.* New York: Harper & Brothers, Franklin Square.

224 / HARMONY OF BABEL

Sebestyén, G. (n.d.). *A Self-Portrait.* (n.p.).

Sugár, A. (1985). *Nyílt titkaim* [My open secrets]. Budapest: Author.

Szacski, T. & Zsuravljova, N. (1988). СЕЙЧАС СКАЖУ! (Orosz társalgás iskolásoknak) [Russian conversation for schoolchildren]. Budapest: Tankönyvkiadó.

Taneda, T. (1969). 20カ国語ペラペラ [Fluency in 20 languages]. Tokyo: Jitsugyo no Nihon Sha.

Tucci, G. (1942). *Alessandro Csoma de Kőrös.* Kolozsvár (today: Cluj-Napoca, Romania): Ferenc József Tudományegyetem [Franz Joseph University].

Vámbéry, Á. (1904). *The story of my struggles: The memoirs of Árminius Vámbéry.* New York: E. P. Dutton and Co.

Watts, T. (1859). On Dr. Russell's life of Cardinal Mezzofanti. *Transactions of the Philological Society,* pp. 227–256.

Appendix:
An Interview with Dr. Kató Lomb

≈

By Tamás Vitray of the Hungarian television program *Ötszem-közt* [Between Five Eyes]. (Between you, me, and the camera). 1974.

Vitray [addressing the camera]: *Now, in an unconventional way, perhaps the dear viewers won't mind my telling you that our guest today is Mrs. Frigyes Lomb (née Kató Szilárd)—otherwise known by her pen name, Dr. Kató Lomb—who speaks 16 languages and is an interpreter at major international conferences.*

Vitray [turning to Dr. Lomb]: *Where are you going next for an international conference?*

Lomb: I have an interesting program in mid-September: I'm invited to The Hague, to a conference on the standardization of artificial insemination.

"The standardization of artificial insemination..." Is it decent to ask how something like that can be standardized?

I don't know yet! Unfortunately—

And how are you preparing?

I hope the "Arbeitsunterlagen"—i.e., the procedure documentation that will help us familiarize ourselves with the vocabulary and the expected direction of the discussion—will arrive in time.

Do you know yet into what language you'll interpret?

Yes. I'll have to interpret French and English into each other. Some delegates will occasionally rise to speak in German or Russian, which I'll also translate into English and French. That is, we'll have four passive and two active languages.

And you'll have to translate into both English and French in parallel?

This is called consecutive interpreting, when we don't speak from a booth, concurrently with the speaker. Instead we wait for the delegates to say whatever they have to say, and we translate afterward. In fact, foreign delegates are rather spoiled. They sometimes speak for four or five minutes without stopping, and at such times the poor interpreters have to keep fairly long passages in their minds.

Do you take notes in such cases?

Yes, I do. I generally use pictograms to take notes.

What does that mean?

It means that I make use of Chinese pictograms, because they're quite concise and—

You note in Chinese whatever you will translate into English and French?

Yes.

I must say I think that's a unique feat.

In fact, ways of note-taking for consecutive interpreting are taught at interpreters' courses at universities abroad, and those methods are quite expedient, too. The symbols they work with are, in effect, almost like Chinese characters.

I may have been misinformed, although I did my best to find out as much as possible. Is it possible that you're self-employed [i.e., as opposed to working for the Communist state]?

We are all self-employed. It's—

"You all"? Who are they?

We who interpret as our full-time occupation.

How is that possible? You are invited to major international conferences, but I suppose you have a number of clients here. You translate—

The turnover is quite high.

As for organizations, do you belong to any?

We couldn't manage it! We tried our best. We feel that it's not a very fortunate situation, but our clients change so frequently that I understand that they prefer to make contracts with us directly, rather than with some intermediary body that happens to have nothing to do with the given topic. Our employer changes three times a week.

In that case let me be cheeky now. If you're self-employed, does it mean that you set your own prices?

Yes, although there is some regulation about it, which means that remuneration is a matter of agreement. Of course, a standard practice or a framework has developed, and it is known to our clients and to us. We tend to undertake jobs by ourselves, partly based on difficulty and partly based on our prospective engagements. Being self-employed, of course, comes with immense drawbacks. For example, we are not entitled to a pension and, even worse, we are excluded from social-security services, which is quite a pressure in today's world, especially for those of us who are [primary] breadwinners and who raise children. Interpreters who provide for their families usually enter the social-security system voluntarily [because their employers do not pay for their social security through paycheck deductions].

Well, this is exactly what I was about to ask: I guessed there must be a way to pay for social security voluntarily.

Yes, this option is available. I did it for a while, I think for three years, but I remained healthy for three years. I got so angry paying for social security without benefits that I quit.

It is like that car insurance ad: "Advising you with caution." A lot of car drivers know that once they stop their insurance, they'll be afflicted with…heaven forbid. I didn't mean it like that.

I have your book here, which helped me prepare: How I Learn Languages. *I think it sold out several printings. How many?*

Two, as of today.

Two. How many copies per printing?

If I remember correctly, around 24,000.

For a single printing? Well, that's a pretty high print run. So you used to be a chemist? That is what your doctorate is in?

Yes, in chemistry and physics.

And why did you give them up?

For two reasons: Chemistry and I didn't like each other. Of course you could ask why I chose it in the first place, because it's a fairly complicated and difficult field of study. Well, there was no career counseling in those days, and I didn't realize my ability and orient myself toward linguistics. The precision and accuracy that are indispensable to chemists were lacking in me. It became evident when we had to take the test tubes in our hands. This was one of the reasons that made me leave chemistry. The other was that when I graduated in the early 1930s, we suffered from such an incredible recession that even older chemists with more experience were left without livelihoods. I, as a novice, was even less likely to get a job. I had fortune in misfortune, however. I reached—

Now you're happy about this turn of events?

I am indeed. You can never know!

You didn't miss chemistry? Still, it must have helped you many times when you translated related topics.

Yes, but unfortunately science as a whole has changed so much in the meantime that these days when I translate chemistry, I cannot make use of my old knowledge. In those times I did analyses with laboratory techniques, such as volumetric and gravimetric analysis, that are non-existent today! These days everything is done with physical or optical methods.

So you had to prepare once again.

Completely.

[Vitray pauses.] Now we're at a point that I believe is common for you: A refreshment is served, but you cannot enjoy it because you have to translate all the time. So I'll take a break now. [Vitray lets her have her coffee.]

I'll have it (laughs). Thank you. It's thoughtful of you.

I'm going to be less thoughtful now. But you'll understand that I'm not asking you so as to make a nuisance of myself. If someone speaks 16 languages, people are inevitably bound to ask if they dare (or if not, they will still wonder) how many of them you studied, as we put it, von Haus aus *[from a nanny] or from a language teacher.*

None.

After all, your father was a doctor, so the presumption of a nanny or tutor is not that far-fetched.

He was a doctor for the poor; we lived in a small city. We were struggling with quite petty financial issues. I didn't study any language as a child…except for French, which I acquired for myself at a middle-school level. Of course, in school I studied Latin as well, which was compulsory in those days. I started my other language studies as an adult, and I like to emphasize it as an encouragement for those who are kept back from studies by the thought of "Oh my God, I'm already x years old." This "x" often begins as early as 30. I am terribly angry at this prejudice. There are three prejudices that I strove to fight in my book. The first is that you can learn languages only as a child or at least at a very young age. The second is that you need a "language talent" to force your way to a particular level. The third is that living abroad is *the* way to acquire a language.

So you're angry with these three prejudices. The first one is that we are able to learn languages only at a young age, with a young mind. Please be so kind as to tell me your counterarguments briefly.

Being able to learn languages only at a young age is the most prevalent prejudice, and probably that's why it is the one I'm the angriest about. You know, I like to divide proficiency into two parts: skill and knowledge. It's quite obvious in other languages, where there is a separate *Fertigkeit* ["skill" in German], which has nothing to do with *Kenntnis* ["knowledge" in German] or *connaissance* ["knowledge" in French]. Now, it's true that a child can acquire a *skill* better than an adult can. Nobody disputes that a six-year-old will more readily learn how to ride a bicycle than will a 60-year-old. However, the other essential is knowledge. A mature head is much more suited to acquire knowledge than is a child's mind. In our trade, pronunciation is the skill, the automatic ability to accomplish something. As far as pronunciation is concerned, there's no debate that an unbiased and unprejudiced young mind will succeed and perform much better than an adult's. It's proven by a million examples that native-like pronunciation cannot be achieved beyond a particular age.

What is your pronunciation like in the languages that you know best?

Unfortunately, it's mediocre! I must admit it. Exactly for the reasons I said previously. I started language learning as an adult. We usually say that the basis of articulation has already calcified by that time. So it's a kind of bottleneck for my abilities. Now, let me turn quickly to the third prejudice.

That is, we can learn a language properly only abroad.

Yes, [but] if you visit a foreign country as an adult, then you start at a bad time in terms of pronunciation: By then the reactions of the speech organs have developed so much that in fact, as we know from the cases of our brothers and sisters who defected [from Hungary to the West], we cannot catch up with the natives.

Just a moment, please. I'm sorry to divert you. This morning I was wondering whether to ask a certain question, but now that you brought it up, I will. You are a genuine expert. What is the reason you called them "our brothers and sisters who defected"? Many times I have met people who left, say, in 1956 [the year of the Hungarian revolt against Soviet rule] but also people who left later. The point is that they speak broken Hungarian. Why? Is it just putting on airs?

No. You say they speak broken *Hungarian*?

Yes, Hungarian! Their mother tongue! In which, as you put it, their basis of articulation had calcified.

No, it's not spontaneous, not at all. They want to impress; this is how they try to make up for their non-existent foreign-language competence. The mother tongue is a skill, and it's a feature of skills that they don't disappear but persist forever. A mother tongue is a skill that cannot be forgotten. I don't believe native language skills fail anyone, even if they stay abroad for 40 years. I could cite a million examples. I can imagine that the people you refer to would need four or five days to get used to reacting automatically in Hungarian and reacting properly. It's just like people who learned how to ride a bicycle. Once they know, they will hardly ever fall off, even if they haven't ridden for 30 years. At most they'll have to focus on balance in the saddle for a while. Losing fluency in Hungarian is mere affectation, nothing else.

And now there is the second prejudice, which you missed.

The issue of language talent. This is, again, one of my archenemies. As a matter of fact, the fight against the need for talent led me to write my book. This hazy and mysterious "language talent" has kept a lot of people from language learning and, as such, it deserved my full wrath. Language talent is something complex, to say the least. On my way here, I remembered a notable Hungarian literary translator. Unfortunately, we lost him about 15 years ago *[actually in 1955, 19 years before the interview—Trans.]*. Endre Gáspár: I suppose you've heard his name, for sure.

Certainly!

He translated Lorca, Béranger, Heine, and Shelley with an

234 / HARMONY OF BABEL

astonishing talent, wonderfully indeed, at an artistic level completely identical to the original. He spoke all these languages; he
spoke all of them equally. In a sense, you could never know which
one he was speaking [because of his Hungarian accent].

*János Arany [a well-known Hungarian poet] is said to have had
horrible pronunciation when he spoke English at all, although it's
hardly possible to translate Shakespeare better than he did.*

Unsurpassable! The difference is that he rarely ever left his
[native] Nagyszalonta, whereas Endre Gáspár wandered the world
as a political émigré, so he'd have had the opportunity to acquire
good pronunciation. But Gáspár's pronunciation was very bad.
I don't know what to call him. A language anti-talent? If I have
a criterion of native-like pronunciation, then I have to call him
"anti." If I consider the way he rendered literature, at a level identical to the original, then I have to say he was a language genius.
This is one of my arguments against [the concept of a language
talent]. My other argument is that people think simultaneous interpreters must be geniuses. Some two or three years ago, two
young boys were competing on a talent show on TV. One had, I
think, South America as his topic, and the other, if I remember
correctly, Somogy County [in Hungary]. It was staggering how
much they knew about these places. Yet, no one said that X was
a "genius" at South America or Y was a "genius" at Somogy. They
were described as intelligent boys who were full of curiosity and
who happened to be driven by bits of information about these
two places. They accomplished impressive results with their open
eyes and their diligence. But folks think we must be geniuses.

So there is no language talent, this kind of specific talent.

There is diligence, motivation, persistence, and knowing how to learn. These qualities are indispensable for studying anything.

What motivated you or what prompted you to choose the Russian language in 1941? The date is not incidental here.[176]

I'd be rather happy to say my decision was ideological and political foresight. But I would be lying. I could almost say it was an accident. I described it in my book. In a downtown second-hand bookstore, I chanced upon a very old Russian-English dictionary, I think from 1880, and I was so enchanted by the Cyrillic alphabet, then unfamiliar to me, that I rushed home with the dictionary and started to pore over it. I had read a lot of Russian literature in translation. I had the impression that whoever is truly interested in matters of psychology will remain uninformed without Dostoyevsky, Tolstoy, Gogol, and Chekhov. I set about learning Russian. On my own. Needless to say, it wasn't quite possible then to study with a teacher in Hungary, which was becoming imbued with fascism. And incidentally, my efforts were rewarded in the weeks of the liberation [winter 1944 to spring 1945]. Oddly enough, I was practically the only one able to type on a Russian typewriter, which had Cyrillic letters. This was my main advantage, which got me hired on February 4, 1945, as the Russian interpreter for the then-mayor.

"You were hired," you said. It means you had applied.

Yes, by myself.

---

176. Vitray is referring to the fact that it was unknown in Hungary in 1941 that the Soviets would liberate the country from the Nazis in 1945 and occupy the country.

You weren't discovered as a speaker of Russian?

No, no! I knocked—

What motivated you to do that?

You won't believe it: The light was on in the room of the mayor's office! It's very difficult to reconstruct now, in July 1974, how extraordinary it was, but just imagine. Budapest was in ruins, and then I saw light in a window.

And you entered just because there was light inside?

I knocked, I introduced myself, and I asked if the mayor's staff needed an interpreter. Whereupon they told me to stop speaking so much, sit down, and phone the city's Soviet commander.

Zamertsev, wasn't he?

Yes, Zamertsev. We became very good friends.

And you picked up the phone and started to speak Russian.

There was one line open in Budapest at that time.

A single phone line?

I even asked them about his number, and they started to laugh. They told me to just pick up the receiver, and they would—

Zamertsev was on the other end.

And so it happened.

And so your motivation to learn Russian paid off, as I suppose your life became stable now thanks to this new and important position.

Russian did give me a leg-up. Not only financially, but my life gained momentum, a kind of drive, a kind of impetus, which hasn't left me even today, and I very much hope it'll stay with me till the last minute of my life.

There is one thing I admired about you, and now I'll step back a little bit in terms of chronology. It may be only my own personal admiration, rather than something general. You write in your book that you studied Russian during the air raid warnings, and what's more, if I recall correctly, you even had to hide the book at the shelter. Well, I really admired you for how you could endure it, to concentrate right in the middle of a bombing.

It's typically a matter of motivation. A truly genuine motivation, a very profound incentive, makes you indifferent toward the dangers of your surroundings.

Weren't you afraid that all the things you were working for might be in vain? That a bomb might explode right there at any moment?

I don't know. A mother won't really give it much thought, either, when she's protecting her child, whether he will become a scoundrel. One is so caught up in this extremely deep motivation (it may be immodest of me to use a comparison like that), but it's a feature of a strong impetus that you won't wonder whether the task is worthy. You know, very often someone will call me, a stranger, and ask "Please tell me, is it worth learning"—I don't know—"Spanish or Chinese?" And I always reply, "Not for you, son." Then a resentful voice counters, "Why are you saying that,

238 / HARMONY OF BABEL

ma'am? You don't even know me, do you?" I tell him that whoever asks the question should not even bother to try! You can't do
it so rigidly, calculating whether learning the language will pay
enough. If you're not inspired by the process itself—well, my message to everyone is that learning a language is so good that it's
worth doing for itself! So if people don't have a sense of mission,
it's no use for them to start. If they set their eyes only on how
profitable it'll turn out to be—

*Well, I studied languages myself, too, albeit with quite minimal
practice. I can say that when you claim that learning languages is
good, I'm not so sure. The result is good: It's a great, fantastic feeling.
But to make language studies good—that is, to find joy in learning
itself—aren't you afraid that one needs to have some kind of disposition, one like yours, for example? In other words, what's the joy in the
process of learning?*

Learning is a joy when you ignore *Homo sapiens*, the wise
man. I don't really believe in this kind of sapience, this wisdom.

We have quite a lot of conflicting data.

Yes! But instead, [one should consider] *Homo ludens*, the play-
loving man. People are quite fond of playing! They enjoy playing
intellectual games, as well as physical games and sports.

How am I supposed to play with language learning?

Language learning is like turning the pages of a puzzle magazine and solving the crosswords. The way for people to find language learning interesting and avoid getting tired, to do it for
hours, is to let it satisfy this particular desire for games, to view it

as a puzzle to be solved. When the pieces fall in place, language gives you an enormous sense of achievement, just like reconciling the horizontal and vertical lines in a crossword puzzle. May I give you an example?

Of course!

I didn't want to exceed the 16 languages I know. I swore to myself that I wasn't going to learn more. However, I happened to have a free month (translating is quite hectic but fluctuating), and I didn't know what to do with my extra time. Once again, I found myself in a second-hand bookstore, and I bought a Swedish novel. Unfortunately, it turned out that it was by a Danish author, Karin Michaëlis, translated into Swedish, but it was too late then; I had invested the five forints already. Well, I started reading the book. After I had finished it, I couldn't even tell what it was about, or whether it had a subject or a heroine. I couldn't possibly orient myself in it. Then I went through it a second time. The context supplied the vocabulary of the whole thing very well, since Swedish resembles English and German quite a lot. It was rather easy to glean the words from it. The grammatical connections are just the same. I read it a third time, and I was fully aware of the book's content and the Swedish grammar. When I started the next book [also Swedish], I even translated it and offered it to Magvető Publishing House for publication. Unfortunately, it turned out that I had reinvented the wheel, as—

It had been translated already.

—it had been translated already.

Now, returning to our topic: You say you took this Swedish book in your hand first, without knowing the pronunciation of Swedish words, without knowing the grammar.

I admit that I'm still not familiar with the pronunciation even now. If I have some motivation to get back to it—

So you need a conference to do that?

A conference, or maybe a friend, to make it worthwhile for his or her sake. Then I'll skim through the rules of pronunciation. Even though my pronunciation will never match a native speaker's, I'll learn how to pronounce that ä with two dots, and then the å, with a diacritical mark of—

A ring.

—a ring, and so on. I'll look these up. At this moment, I have a clear view of the grammar rules, I can enjoy works of literature, I can translate—

You found out these grammar rules from this very novel? You "abstracted" them?

This is the only way. This is the only way to do it. Otherwise it would be boring. If I had taken a grammar book, my sense of duty would have kept me with it for maybe half an hour, but then I'd have gotten bored to death with it, and I'd have tossed it against the wall and read a good novel.

But do be completely honest: If you hadn't known any other foreign languages, and you had started this Swedish book as you say, you'd have hardly gotten through it. You couldn't have read it without comparing it to other languages.

You're very much right, yes. I'm convinced that I can't really perceive a phenomenon of grammar, lexicon, or meaning without making an analogy to something I already know. It has taken me the long diligence of my life to make such connections. Nevertheless, I believe that we should push bilingual books. There is a trade-off here, for when we translate such books and wish to make them enjoyable as literature, we are practically obliged to depart from the original language so much that the translation can hardly be used as a key to learning the source language.

I'm very angry with the common use of the dictionary: Once you come across an unknown word, you quickly look it up and check it out. I'm angry for two reasons: First, it slows the process of reading so much that it discourages people, and they can't wait to throw away the book. Second, using a dictionary is so superficial; looking up words lacks a sense of achievement so much that these words will go out of one's mind quickly. It's only at the start that I suggest that everyone use the dictionary to get acquainted with the language and glean the rules from the phrases. But if you want to derive grammar itself, to abstract it, note that Toussaint–Langenscheidt said *"Man lernt Grammatik aus der Sprache, nicht Sprache aus der Grammatik."* One learns grammar from language, not language from grammar. It was terrible, this old method of education, based on the instruction of Greek and Latin. Students were fed the entire grammatical system and then expected to know how to converse.

Now we have reached another point. You imply that it's the sense of achievement that makes language learning so inspiring. And I believe that! However, most people need to study a language with a teacher [to get results]. And I must say it's not a compliment. If you study on your own, you need to have a certain disposition that will give you a sense of achievement—the same feeling you get when you read [and solve] a puzzle magazine. For all practical purposes, language teachers, if they teach well, actually deprive you of a sense of achievement. It's a strange paradox, and yet it's true.

It's true.

Teachers are supposed to call attention to my mistakes! But if I am making mistakes, they can't tell me I am learning a language well.

That's why they are educators: to tell you your mistakes. Unfortunately, it's true.

One of our leading politicians recently asked me to escort him to a country whose language I spoke very poorly. I had only two months to get ready.

Though I appreciate your discretion, you should at least name the country.

O.K., I'll say *(laughs)*. It was a Spanish-speaking country. Well, I had two options: I could have called upon a Spanish teacher (there are a number of talented ones in Hungary) to instruct me. But I was afraid that—because of the nature of their profession—they would always warn me about whatever I said wrongly. So I dismissed this solution. I bought a book. I call it women's pulp fiction, so it's not men's fiction, not a detective story.

A crime story.

Not a crime story, which we women have less flair for. I read through a good book of women's pulp fiction. Spanish is not difficult. I must say it closely resembles Latin, French, and Italian. And I escorted this comrade without having taken a single class. Well, they found my pronunciation a bit…strange, but I survived my long stay very well.

So you insist on a sense of achievement. Well, it's very difficult to protect yourself [against constant correction by teachers]. In classroom language teaching (not to mention private and group classes), the sense of achievement is inevitably sacrificed on the one hand for the grading system, and on the other hand for the obligation to correct mistakes, rather than emphasize the positives.

That is why my method is often scoffed at as an out-of-school and even no-teacher kind of language learning. Instead, I'd rather say it's the method of impatient people. And impatience is something extremely healthy in language learning.

It is my conviction that one cannot achieve good results in language learning without investing 12 to 14 hours a week. In fact, that amount of time is fairly difficult to manage with an educator for various reasons, including financial ones. It doesn't work—let's be honest. So even if students let themselves be guided by a teacher (and I admit you're right that the vast majority do), they need to bolster themselves through self-study to supplement this minimal number of classes. And the need for supplementing is why I emphasize the importance of reading so much. I'm not saying that reading is the most efficient way to learn a language. It would be absurd. We know from Pavlov that multipronged motivation—activating several approaches—leads to the best results. Reading focuses on visuals only, the text. It lacks the emotional impulse present in a personal encounter, such as a conversation with a friend. So reading is one-sided and less efficient. However, printed words are highly accessible; they can be acquired by very simple and cheap means. I don't believe anyone is so terribly busy that he or she can't spend one or two hours a day reading. And reading can fit into one's schedule so well—for example, when traveling or when eating breakfast or dinner.

Have you ever taught?

I tried twice, always in cases when there was no one more qualified and suited than I was. One was when Russian instruction was introduced [in Hungary in 1949]. I taught for a year at the [Budapest] University of Technology, where I could put my memories of physics to good use. The other was when the Society for Dissemination of Scientific Knowledge was started. They offered a Chinese course, but our Chinese scholarship recipients [teachers] hadn't come yet. Once they arrived, I was happy to pass this job on to them.

And in these two cases, did you make any changes to your method? In comparison to the usual, traditional teaching methods?

I applied my own method 100%! I immediately started to teach technical literature to my student friends. They liked it a lot; I am glad it has since become a common method. These days instructors very early switch to teaching youth what they're interested in. Indeed, it's only logical for would-be chemical engineers to take an interest in the vocabulary of their profession.

In the current international situation, I think, interactions are steadily on the rise. I can safely say that, without having counted them, all signs indicate this rise. Will an interpreter's—a multilingual interpreter's—vocation experience a boom?

It won't, unfortunately.

Why?

You're perfectly right that relations are consolidating, broadening, and deepening, but from a linguist's point of view, we are witnessing an interesting process, which I'd call, if not integration, at least polarization. To be more precise, today two poles have developed. English and Russian serve as common languages in international communication to an extent that is quite shocking. As a matter of fact, sometimes it makes me sigh when I wonder what will become of interpreting, which has grown rather close to my heart, needless to say.

I had an astonishing experience. Last week, a conference on microwave transmission took place here in Budapest. It was large, with five hundred delegates from 33 countries, if I recall correctly. These specialists made themselves understood in English so well! I'm not saying their English was excellent. I think they would have gotten a C from a strict high school teacher. They used bad sentence construction, bad grammar, and bad pronunciation. But their expertise helped them so much in understanding each other. Their expertise was also reflected in their visual aids: figures, slides, diagrams, everything. These aids contributed so much to their mutual understanding that we interpreters just kept sighing, sitting in the corner.

Was it embarrassing?

It was more like we were grieving, yes, because we were wondering what would become of our trade, after all.

Then let's have a closer look at this trade now, if you'll help me.

A short while ago you taught me a term: You said "consecutive interpreter." I know there are simultaneous interpreters and there are accompanying interpreters. I've heard that you call the latter "chanters" [i.e., rattling off information in a sing-song manner]. Is that true?

We very much respect accompanying interpreters, and we're very sad that they don't get the financial and intellectual recognition that they deserve. Just consider a stranger who arrives here in Hungary, with its 10 million inhabitants. He'll have permanent contact with only one person: the accompanying interpreter. Now, it's a common human frailty for him or any of us to think that a country is like that single person (or a handful of people at best) whom we personally meet. So much is expected then from an accompanying interpreter! Language skills—

Still, why did this somewhat derogatory term "chanters" take root among simultaneous and other learned interpreters? You eluded it very aptly, with a great sense of diplomacy. If it's not like that, then I was misinformed. But I believe they are a bit looked down on within the trade.

We are angry at accompanying interpreters because they don't assert themselves properly. This is our sole charge against them: that they resign themselves to the fact that they are many and that they don't manage to gain the financial and intellectual recognition that we do. I must say—

Why are you angry at them when simultaneous interpreters such as yourself have succeeded?

We'd like to improve their status. We see them as our colleagues, and we'd like them to feel that they do an invaluable job.

In some aspects what they do is more than what we do, although we do a much harder job. Booth interpreting is such an interesting and extraordinary form of cognitive functioning that it deserves all its recognition. I can say that—

Well, maybe I'm being nasty now, but is it possible that you have a bias against accompanying interpreters because you feel discredited in some way? Because they are generally too cheaply available?

You've been dealing with the matter for only five or 10 minutes, but you give evidence of quite amazing acumen.

Oh, no. I just reworded what you said. I was interpreting things, so to speak, into my own professional jargon.

You drew the conclusions excellently. There is a kind of social condescension toward interpreters, as it were. Somehow we are not truly accepted either as experts or as specialists. It is somewhat explained by the fact that we're actually identified with those who work for pennies [accompanying interpreters]. I must say pennies because, in comparison to their skills and performance, it's only pennies that they receive. [But then] accompanying interpreters do tend to mechanically rattle off words.

They "chant."

You said it.

No, I've heard it!

They rattle off whatever they have to say, and this shadow is cast on us, too. Even 10 years ago, before arriving in Hungary, a delegate would ask for an interpreter in his or her list of contract riders. The list would read something like this: "manicure—pedi-cure—interpreter."

It's rather offensive, isn't it?

Highly. Indeed, we're fighting for intellectual recognition at least as much as for financial recognition. We [simultaneous in-terpreters] have elevated ourselves from the class of accompanying interpreters.

To avoid generalizations about our work, all translators should act with more self-respect. I admit our profession includes mem-bers who do not exactly deserve appreciation in terms of political loyalty. We have such members because the need for interpreters is so great that state and business concerns cannot always select for maximum intelligence, political solidity, and other qualities, such as diligence, penchant for working, etc. Still, it's a very decent bunch of people!

Is it the Kató Lomb team?

We can call it whatever.

That's what it's called, isn't it? Isn't that official?

No, no. I'd refuse it. These days I can generally handle fewer matters of organization.

But this [the Kató Lomb team] is what they call themselves. Now I'm embarrassed because I thought it was an official designation.

No. I'd very much object to it. Usually people who have an excess of time do such organizing. There's a core of simultaneous interpreters who are primarily featured at international confer-

ences. The core expands (or not) depending on how many conferences coincide. Unfortunately, a large number of them do coincide. If I may voice a complaint here and exploit the popularity of
Between Five Eyes, there are two seasons when conferences are held
in Hungary, spring and fall. It results in sometimes three, four,
or five highly important conferences coinciding, and we and the
organizers really have to rush to satisfy the demands. Then there
is a long winter sleep and a summer "hibernation," so to speak,
when there is nothing.

*Sometimes these meetings coincide. I think that's how it can be
ensured that a large number of interpreters will be on hand.*

This is what the organizers say, too.

*They do, don't they? Acting like that might come across as a cer-
tain maliciousness [favoring the practical side of arranging conferences without considering the toll on the interpreters they depend on].
The organizers say that it's difficult to get into this rather élite
circle of interpreters. Please forgive my audaciousness in saying so, but
I believe it is especially difficult for young people to enter this circle.*

Tamás, do you remember tokens on trams?

I remember them very well!

You could buy the token only on the tram, but you couldn't
take a tram without having a token. My point is that only an
interpreter with practice is good enough to work in the booth,
but practice can be acquired only in the booth. We, too, feel the
contradiction [as young people who want to enter the profession
do], but we don't really know the remedy. Just imagine how dif-

ficult it is for the head of an interpreting team to hire someone who might quit in the first quarter-hour. Isn't it logical, then, that we prefer to work with people, and mobilize people, who have proven that they are able to cope with all the contingencies and difficulties? Our difficulties are enormous. Just think of the fact that even though there are schools for interpreters, there are no schools for the people we interpret. No one has taught delegates that we cannot interpret them if they speak very fast or if they speak a language other than their native tongue with very bad pronunciation. Sometimes they read a text prepared in advance, but often we see that text only at the last minute. We do have to tackle a big handicap indeed.

Isn't there an opportunity for some kind of prior discussion between the interpreter and the person interpreted?

Our delegates are vain. If approached beforehand, they'll often just say "Oh, I'm going to improvise." Yet when they're up on stage, they'll quickly pull a sheet of paper from their pocket. They jabber at such a rate that one just keeps grabbing for the predicate, without which, as it is well known, we interpreters cannot start translating anything.

Have you ever stopped translating because of a speaker's jabbering? And has the speaker ever noticed it and understood that he should repeat his words?

We've even asked the chair to admonish the delegate to speak a little slower. There are other methods [for slowing the speaker], too: The interpreter can turn on a red light or press a buzzer to indicate problems. It's a funny psychological phenomenon that if the red light goes on, which is the agreed signal for "Oh, we can't translate at this rate," then for some reason it just urges the speakers to speed up even more.

They think they have to hurry up!

They do! It's such an international finding that we've given up the red light already. It's impossible.

To my knowledge, in large international organizations, such as maybe the U.N. and related organizations, interpreters are supposed to be at least natively bilingual. That is, they should, by luck of birth, have two native languages: a "mother tongue" and a "father tongue" [their mother's and father's respective native languages or another two or three languages acquired in different social environments].

Yes.

They can translate from one to the other, but they are not usually allowed to use languages they learned academically [after childhood].

No, they aren't allowed. U.N. rules are much stricter than ours. We are a small country; here we cannot stick to those rather rigid regulations.

Then what is the reason that, according to my information, you and your team were invited to more than one international conference? There would have been competitors in father and mother tongues there.

We have more enthusiasm, more penchant for the work. We are happier to do it, and we don't have the kind of indifference that has developed, unfortunately, in our foreign colleagues.

Is it because your foreign colleagues are paid worse? Is that possible?

They receive fantastic amounts. Well, I can tell you on *Between Five Eyes* that, at this moment, they earn around 130 dollars a day [in 2018 dollars, about 680]. Even so, their international organization [AIIC: International Association of Conference Interpreters] has such strict regulations that many foreign interpreters won't take anything that is not a booth job. So if they've spent a day interpreting in the booth and afterward they're asked to appear at a banquet and to translate the inviter's words—such as "I warmly welcome the delegates; enjoy your meal"—they're not allowed to undertake it.

Another interpreter will have to be hired for that?

[Yes, because] it is outside the [AIIC] interpreter's line of duty, and he or she will say no. We are popular because we more strongly identify with the organizers. I dare to claim this about the [Hungarian] team members: We don't consider ourselves as auxiliaries hired case-by-case for two or three days, but as the linguistic experts of the event. Before it, during it, and in fact very often even after it, we are caught up in the topic.

Do these events ever have nothing to do with Hungary?

I'm very often abroad without having any fellow Hungarians with me, or even anybody from a fellow Democratic People's Republic. I frankly admit that on these occasions I'll somewhat long for someone beside me in the booth who is not just a mere delegate. But it very often happens that there is no one.

Are you a member of this AIIC?

No, an interpreter from a Democratic People's Republic[177] cannot be a member. Among other reasons, because of the membership fees. It's a fairly big amount, which should be paid in dollars, and we can't really—

Can't it be paid from what you receive as income from these engagements?

It can't, and there is another difficulty as well. As I said, regulations are very strict. For example, we wouldn't be allowed [by the AIIC] to do interpreting for less than 130 dollars a day. This rate of pay would hardly be possible in Hungary.

You couldn't work for less than 130 dollars a day in Hungary?

If we were regular members, then we couldn't. And there is another reason for us not to join: It's a body specifically for the protection of interests. If membership enabled us [Hungarian interpreters] to further develop and learn the theoretical aspects of our trade, then we'd perhaps [be encouraged to] lobby our financial authorities [for greater compensation]. Because membership is purely for the protection of interests, and because there is such a big gap between our customs and those abroad, we resolved not to join the AIIC.

Then who will protect your interests?

The demand! It's not quite in line with the Marxist approach, but unfortunately there is a certain demand, and there is a definite

---

177. I.e., a Communist country.

supply. This proportion allows us to receive, first of all, financial compensation and, second, the intellectual recognition that I feel our work deserves.

Please feel free not to answer this question if it goes beyond the limits of what I may ask you on television. But you told me what interpreters earn abroad, and you've mentioned foreign pay rates. This encourages me to ask: What do you find appropriate in terms of financial compensation here? And what does that imply?

At this moment, the fee for interpreters is around 700, 750, 800 forints on average per day, which may sound very nice if you do not consider the fact that it's preceded by preparation, sometimes for a month but sometimes for half a year.

So it doesn't just mean that single day when you work.

I could almost say that you've done most of your work by the time you sit in the booth. Once a Swiss company organized a conference on potassium. For three long days, we spoke about nothing but potassium. Imagine the preparation!

But it's related to your field!

To mine, yes. But there were lawyers and doctors among us, and people of other backgrounds. Just imagine what intensive study it took us [the interpreters, to prepare for the conference]. And where do you need to begin such study? In fact, you must start with your high school knowledge and proceed gradually to university-level knowledge and even beyond, because the material at that conference will not be taught even in universities for years.

There is actually only one more thing that intrigues me. If there's anything else you'd enjoy talking about, please tell me. From listening to all the things you've said—on the one hand, about language learning, and on the other hand, about your vocation, which is interpreting—I came to the conclusion that language is your passion and your hobby. So maybe it will not sound too banal if I ask, Are you entirely happy and content? Have you "actualized" yourself, as one would put it in a fashionable way?

I'd say 80%.

Then what is the 20%?

Look, if I may complain a bit on television: There is a problem here in Hungary; it may exist in other countries as well. Everyone has an assigned and rather fixed role to play. I've been given the role of chief polyglot in Hungary, and society expects me to fulfill it. But I can't actualize myself beyond that. It was logical that after dealing with language learning intensively, I would explore the ability to create. What I find terribly intriguing is the nature of the creative individual and the relationship between creation and motivation. This is what I'm engaged in; this is what I'm currently writing a book about. And I'm sad that I'll never find a publisher for it, precisely because in Hungary I'm not the "executive" of this trade, so to speak. But to move to a narrower sphere: I'd like to make a distinction between practicing linguists and theoretical linguists. To the practicing linguist, which I typically represent here in our small country, I apply the term "linguaphile," which simply means someone who knows and speaks many languages. In contrast, theoretical linguists may not be able to speak many languages actively, but they notice theoretical relationships that are immensely exciting and interesting. But theory is still not my trade. No matter how hard I keep trying, theory is not my role. And that's where the 20% lies, which sometimes makes me sigh.

Then again, I think if people can say they found meaning in most of their life, and this meaning fulfills them, it is OK. Meaning is a big deal. [But] meaning may be so distant from younger viewers' minds that they're not concerned about it yet. But intellectual curiosity is a companion that will go with you your whole life as long as you can use your eyes and mind.

So if I understand you well, the 20% implies that you can't satisfy your intellectual curiosity about creativity and get your ideas to the appropriate audience? Because the roles have been assigned [by society]—

It's the second part that I emphasize, that I cannot get my ideas to the public. Of course nobody prevents me from continuing to collect data for a future book [even though it won't be published]. But all interpreters are extroverts, and they like to impart whatever they know. We have been trained by our profession to impart whatever is inside us.

To display—

To display oneself: It's instinctively present in people. I'm no different. I don't want to write two or three books and then put them in a drawer where they will be eventually swept out or burned by my heirs.

Now I remember the article you mentioned.[178] *Was it Saint-Paul-de-Vence?*

---

178. The article is not mentioned by name in the interview.

Yes, it was!

Please tell us about the article. I think it's quite relevant here.

I was invited to a conference on food in Paris. I did what I normally do: I stayed there for a little while after the end of the conference. The main attraction [for me] was a little town in Provence, Saint-Paul-de-Vence, which has a wonderful museum called *Musée imaginaire* [today: Fondation Maeght]. Literally it would be translated as "imaginary museum," but what it means is actually more like "ideal museum." I went there practically on foot, splitting my journey into small legs, just to see the museum. I was not disappointed. I wrote an article about it; I had the feeling my piece was well done. Well, I can proudly say that there was no publisher, no newspaper in Hungary that didn't reject it.

On what grounds?

By saying that I should instead give an interview on how to learn languages. Because that's the role assigned to me!

You're not the only one, I think, to have been assigned a role.

Unfortunately.

It's difficult to get out of a pigeonhole.

I don't exactly know how it works for actresses, but I think it's difficult for a comedienne to reinvent herself as a tragedienne. She won't be accepted.

Well, in that case one's [surface] disposition is quite decisive, too. It was exactly here in this room that I had [the actress] Mari Töröcsik as a guest not very long ago. She told me that in productions these days she's the "tired workwoman" and the "proletarian woman" in charge, although her [actual] disposition would make her suited to several other roles as well. You must have a more difficult task because of your intellectual pursuits.

This profession may actually be what my intellectual disposition predisposes me for. And one will always have misgivings, such as I may not be suitable; maybe someone else should shed light on the theoretical relationships [in language], not me; maybe someone else should write this book. In other words, the sense of achievement—

But you'll write it?

I will, although the sense of achievement is lacking, and uncertainty slows down the pace very much.

What you said makes it quite evident—and this is what I'm ultimately interested in, as it is relevant here—that you keep your mind in shape constantly, no matter if it's the season for interpreting. If it isn't, then you explore creativity and the person who creates—or something else. But I wonder if we become one-sided if we spend all our time on mental activity.

Even this circle is too wide: spending all one's time on mental activity. You need to choose a monomania within the circle of the mind. This monomania can be rather narrow, or it can be somewhat wider, as in my case. I like monomaniacs very much. The opposite is not polymania but indifference. I can't bear indifferent people; they have no place among human beings. But I have a hunch that you want to shed light on another side of the issue:

that one should also maintain one's physical condition in parallel.

Do you have a monomania of this sort as well?

I do. I often describe myself as someone with three obsessions: reading, walking in nature, and skiing *["lektúra, natúra, sítúra"—a wordplay between Latin and Hungarian—Trans.]*. Well, I pursue all three with extraordinary passion. At this point, let me return to the beginning of our conversation, the second of the major language prejudices.

—that above a certain age [one can't learn a language]—

People will accept it so readily, out of comfort or laziness, saying "Oh, I'm too old to do this or that." Even if it's true that it's better to stay in training than to start over again, let's not be so undemanding toward ourselves! Our lifespans have already become so long: We don't die at the age of 40, as in the time of Francis Rákóczi [in the 17th–18th century], but 30 or 40 years later. Then why do we shorten our active period at the end? Why do we give up physical exercise? Or—I'm sorry to use an English word here—give up the "challenge" implied in some new study material. Why do we give it up just because, according to the calendar, we've reached an age that our ancestors viewed as our twilight years?

What does this challenge mean to you in terms of physical training?

Well, I usually ski in all of January, which is, as I said, the most dead month of the year.

The dead month is not so much of a problem, after all!

It's a really joyful recreation. If snow conditions in Hungary don't allow me, I'll go to the Tatra Mountains, where I have a short, well-trodden ski route of my own, so to speak. And since I live at the foot of the Buda Hills, one or two hours of walking is my routine if I happen to have had a very difficult—

Any other sports?

I do gymnastics very intensively.

Alone? As you do languages?

No, thanks to the local councils, there are two or three "household gymnastics groups" in every district. It's a kind of euphemism for the fact that the age range of the gymnastics group does not end at 20 or 30 or even 40, but goes on. It's intensive. We have 90 minutes of exercise a week, which I inexpressibly enjoy. I am convinced that there is mind-body interaction, called psychophysical interaction. Exercise helps me with my intellectual job, and this very intensive intellectual strain helps me with improving my physical condition, too.

Well, I'll thank you for your visit. As you put it, I hope I'm not the only one [who is grateful for having Dr. Lomb as a guest]. I've already learned to love reading and nature. As far as skiing is concerned, I don't think I'll try it because—I don't mean to annoy you—I believe I'm already a bit too old.

I didn't manage to convince you?

Maybe I'll try it some day. Luckily there are so few places [in Hungary] with enough snow [for skiing]. Thank you very much!

Thank you very much.